# THE FIRST PEOPLES OF THE NORTHEAST

# Time Line: First Peoples of the Northeast

## Major Developments in the Northeast

| | *Paleo Period* | *Archaic Period* | |
| --- | --- | --- | --- |
| | | EARLY | MIDDLE |
| **Environment** | Tundra | Nut-bearing forests | |
| **Methods of Obtaining and Preparing Food** | Hunting with spear   Gathering roots, plants | Hunting with spear/atlatl. Gathering roots, plants, nuts, berries. Fishing with nets, spears. Shellfish gathering. Seal hunting on shore. | |

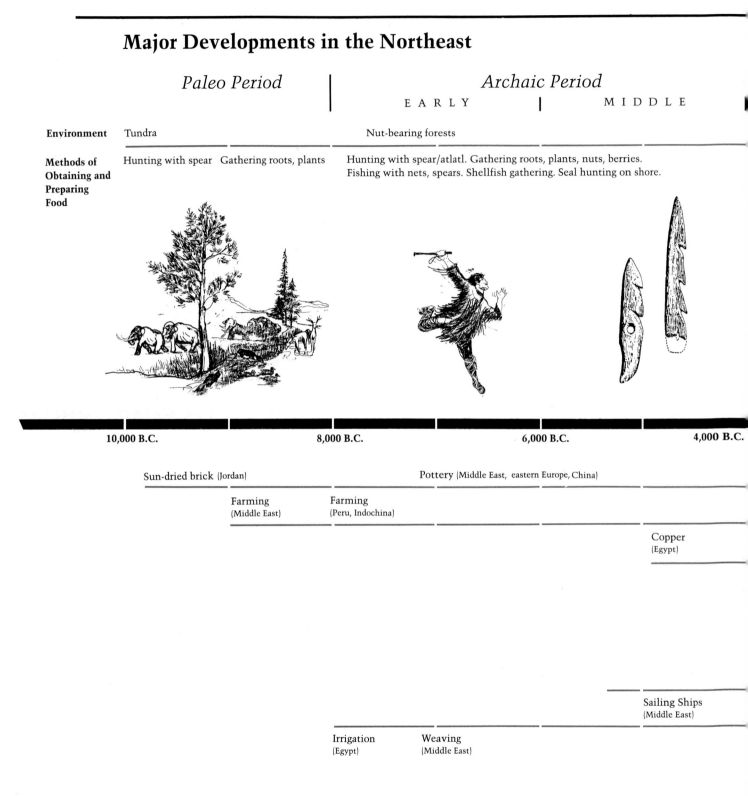

| 10,000 B.C. | 8,000 B.C. | 6,000 B.C. | 4,000 B.C. |
| --- | --- | --- | --- |
| Sun-dried brick (Jordan) | | Pottery (Middle East, eastern Europe, China) | |
| | Farming (Middle East)   Farming (Peru, Indochina) | | |
| | | | Copper (Egypt) |
| | | | Sailing Ships (Middle East) |
| | Irrigation (Egypt)   Weaving (Middle East) | | |

## Major Developments in the Rest of the World

## Archaic Period
### LATE

## Woodland Period
### EARLY | MIDDLE | LATE

Steadily warming climate

Stabilized climate

Hunting with spear/atlatl. Gathering roots, plants, nuts, berries, fruit.
Deep sea fishing and hunting. Fishing with hook, line, net, weirs.
Cooking in soapstone bowls.

Cooking in pottery

Hunting
with
bow
and
arrow

Farming

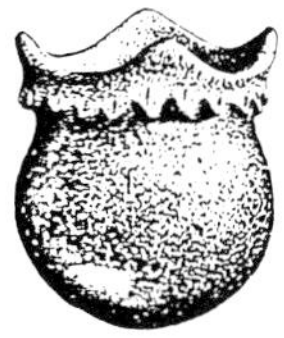

**Contact
with
Europeans**

| 2,000 B.C. | 0 | A.D. 2,000 |
|---|---|---|

Pottery (Central America)

Plow
(China)

Bronze (Middle East) · Iron (Egypt) · Glass (Middle East) · Steel (India)

First Written Language (Sumeria) · Alphabet (Middle East) · Printing (Germany)

First City (Ur) · Pyramids (Egypt) · Greek City States

Rome founded · Mayan culture (Central America) · Incan culture (South America)

Great Wall (China)

Wheel (Middle East) · Vikings (Greenland) · European Explorers

Twelve thousand years ago the first peoples of the
Northeast found a cold and barren landscape in which
to live. As they followed the seasonal movements of
their game, they sheltered themselves in simple windbreaks made of brush and animal skins.

# THE FIRST PEOPLES OF THE NORTHEAST

Esther K. Braun

David P. Braun

## Lincoln Historical Society
Lincoln, Massachusetts

Supported by
Massachusetts Archaeological Society

For further information contact:
Lincoln Historical Society
P.O. Box 84
Lincoln Center, Massachusetts 01773-6084

Frontispiece: Drawing by William Parsons of the Adkins Site in Maine (Figure 12), courtesy of Richard M. Gramly.

Book Design by David Ford

Printed in the United States of America

Library of Congress Cataloging-in-Publication Data

Braun, Esther K. (Esther Kaplan), 1926-
    The first peoples of the Northeast / Esther K. Braun, David P. Braun.
        p.   cm.
    "Supported by Massachusetts Archaeological Society."
    Includes bibliographical references and index.
    ISBN 0-944856-04-7 (acid-free paper) : $18.95 (est.)
    1. Indians of North America--East (U.S.)--Antiquities.
    2. Indians of North America--East (U.S.)--History.
    3. East (U.S.)--Antiquities.  I. Braun, David P.  II. Title.
E78.E2B73   1994                              93-49328
974.01--dc20                                  CIP

To Alanna, Lucas, Jacob, and Doria

# Contents

# Figures and Tables

# Acknowledgments

This book has a long history. It is impossible to thank all who have helped by their interest, encouragement, and suggestions, but three people deserve specific mention. Dr. Elizabeth A. Little, past President of the Massachusetts Archaeological Society and current editor of the Society's Bulletin, gave us her continuous support from the birth of our project, made her own knowledge and professional library available to us, and assisted us in making use of the Society's extensive resources. The encouragement and assistance of Dr. Lynne P. Sullivan, Chair of the Anthropological Survey of the New York State Museum, Albany, New York, greatly helped move the project closer to completion. John C. MacLean, President of the Lincoln Historical Society, Lincoln, Massachusetts, provided editorial advice and coordinated the project for the Historical Society. The book could not have happened without the help of these three fine individuals and their institutions.

Many people reviewed drafts of the text along the way. Among them were Dr. Dena F. Dincauze, Department of Anthropology, University of Massachusetts, Amherst; Dr. Victoria Bunker, then Director of Educational Programs in Archaeology, New Hampshire Historical Society; Barbara Robinson, Dr. Shirley Blancke, and Carole Dwyer, who were then working together on the Concord River Basin Project for the Concord (Massachusetts) Museum and preparing The Native American Sourcebook for Teachers; Emily Herman; Dr. Roger Moeller, then Director of Research for the American Indian Archaeological Institute (now the Institute for American Indian Studies), Washington, Connecticut; Trudy Lamb Richmond, Director of Education at the Institute for American Indian Studies; and Linda Coombs, Native American Program Developer at the Children's Museum in Boston, Massachusetts and Supervisor of Material Culture at Plimouth Plantation, Plymouth, Massachusetts; Dr. Nina Versaggi, Public Archaeology Facility, Binghamton University, Binghamton, New York; Mary Ellen Munley, Chief of Education, New York State Museum, Albany, New York. Dr. Dean R. Snow, Department of Anthropology, State University of New York at Albany, reviewed the materials presented in Appendix B, and gave advice on several maps. So many other archaeologists and educators have given us their support and advice, that we can only thank them as a group. Their enthusiasm helped keep us going and their knowledge helped keep our words accurate and honest.

The illustrations come from many sources, as indicated in the text and in the list of illustration credits. Almost all of the original drawings are by Carole Cote. Dr. Walton C. Galinat, world renowned expert on the evolution of corn, personally contributed copies of his drawings of teosinte, flint corn, and modern corn. Constance Russell delivered by hand the original maps of the trade networks in New England from her father's book, *Indian New England Before the Mayflower*. The rest of the maps were drawn by Betsy Pillsbury. For their generosity with photographs and help in locating others, we also thank Phyliss Steele, Historical Collection Coordinator of The New England; Diane Kopec, Director and former Curator of the Abbe Museum of Stone Age Antiquities, Bar Harbor, Maine; Dr. Richard M. Gramly, formerly at the Buffalo (New York) Museum of Science; Dr. Nicholas Bellantoni and Carl Rettemeyer at the Connecticut State Museum of Natural History; Dr. Mima Kapches and Naomi Jhirad at the Royal Ontario Museum, Toronto; Dr. Priscilla Renouf and Dr. Ingeborg Marshall at the Memorial University, St. John's, Newfoundland; Jane Sproul Thomson, Curator of Archaeology and Ethnology, Government of Newfoundland and Labrador; Tom Lux, Director of the Massachusetts Archaeological Society's Robbins Museum, Middleboro, Massachusetts; Marie Pelletier at Plimouth Plantation, Plymouth, Massachusetts; Dr. Marjorie Power of the

Department of Anthropology, University of Vermont, Burlington; Mr. John Bardwell at Media Services, Dimond Library, University of New Hampshire, Durham; Dr. David Sanger of the Department of Anthropology, University of Maine, Orono; Elizabeth L. Robins, Registrar at the Buffalo Museum of Science; and the New York State Museum, Albany. Christina Rieth assembled and arranged for the photographing of the artifacts from the collections of the New York State Museum and Lisa Anderson was responsible for the completion of that project.

Sue Ann Kearns deserves a special award for her patience and tenacity in typing from the handwritten first draft. It is a marvel that she was able to decipher our two very distinct styles of writing! Special mention goes to the 1980-1981 fourth and fifth grade classes at Hartwell School, Lincoln, Massachusetts, who reluctantly parted with their teacher for half a year to begin the project. They were extremely interested in the process, and even today many continue to ask about its progress. Those who know of its completion are thrilled to have been there at its inception. Many thanks are due to the School Committee of the Lincoln, Massachusetts, Public Schools for approving the semi-sabbatical. A small grant from the Southern Illinois University at Carbondale, Illinois, Office of Research Development and Administration, and the patience of the word processing staff at that University's Center for Archaeological Investigations, made it possible to bring the manuscript into the electronic age.

The design and layout of our book was created by David Ford and the computer files converted and electronically typeset by Mary Ann Hales of the Cottage Press. Together they have been responsible for shepherding the final stages of the publication process. Both are Lincoln residents, which has meant that the book has been "all in the family." We are deeply grateful for their dedication and attention to every detail.

And to our families, our deepest thanks for your support, patience, and helpful suggestions.

# THE FIRST
# PEOPLES
# OF THE
# NORTHEAST

# Introduction

Until the late 1400s, most people living in Europe thought the world was flat and consisted of their continent, Asia, and Africa. When Christopher Columbus sailed from Spain in 1492, he thought that the world was round and that, by sailing west, he would reach land again on the eastern shore of Asia. The land he encountered on his voyages in the 1490s, however, was not Asia but the Americas. As a result, Europeans expanded their world to include this "new" land, which they considered their "New World." The Americas were new only to them, however. Others had discovered and settled these lands thousands of years before.

Today a great deal can be learned about the people of earlier times by studying the written records they left behind. Indeed, ever since people have known how to write, they have left some record of their past. Even old written lists—perhaps lists of the materials people traded, the passengers who sailed on ships, or the citizens of a town—tell much about life in their day. Such records, written by the European explorers and early settlers of the New World, and, therefore, often imperfect or incomplete, have been used to learn about the land and the peoples of the Americas.

Many ancient people developed ways to record their ideas and histories using letters, pictures, or other kinds of symbols. The oldest writings with letters were made around 3,000 B.C., nearly 5,000 years ago, in Mesopotamia (now Iraq). People in ancient China, Egypt, and Central America developed ways of writing with picture-like symbols, called pictographs, almost as long ago. In many parts of the world, though, including North America, people did not keep records until much later. Yet humans have lived on Earth for more than four million years. We have no written records for most of this immense past.

Even if they left no written records, ancient people have always left other materials from which people today can learn about their ways of life. They have left

their worn-out tools, their buildings—sometimes just as they last used them, other times only in ruins—and other physical traces of their lives. When these remains are found today, and carefully treated, they can be fitted together to give a picture of life in the distant past. This way of learning about the past is known as "archaeology."

Archaeology is a science devoted to answering questions about the past. Archaeologists uncover evidence of ancient people—such as their tools, buildings, artwork, and trash—which they study to learn about a people's way of life. The evidence is always incomplete, scattered, broken, and changed by time, so archaeologists' descriptions of the past can never be as complete as we would like. Archaeologists also must take care not to let their ideas reach too far beyond the evidence, to ask questions that it can never answer. After all, how much could we learn about even our own society, if all we had to study were our tools, buildings, artwork, and trash? Archaeologists and others who study the past also can disagree about what the evidence tells us. By gathering more evidence and studying the evidence more, however, archaeologists constantly try to improve our knowledge of the past.

Archaeologists call the places where they find ancient remains, "sites." There are many kinds of archaeological sites. A site could be a place where a woman left her grinding stones or a child dropped a pot; it might be where a group camped for a single night, where several groups gathered in the autumn for many years to catch fish, or where a village once stood; or it could be a cemetery or other sacred place. Archaeologists can learn about the past from almost any kind of site. In recent years, however, archaeologists have come to realize that ancient sacred places remain sacred to living descendants of the people who first used these places. Laws in the United States and in many other countries now protect ancient sacred sites from disturbance, whether by bulldozers or archaeologists.

Laws now also require that remains removed from sacred places be returned to the people whose ancestors used these places. (In several places in this book, you will learn about instances where archaeologists have studied sacred sites. The archaeologists who studied these sites did so before our laws changed to protect such sites, or they did so to rescue knowledge from a site before it was destroyed by construction work.)

Archaeologists have many ways to tell the age of a site. (You can read about these methods, in Appendix A.) The most ancient sites are found only in Africa. Scientists conclude from this evidence that the earliest humans lived only in Africa, between four and five million years ago and perhaps even earlier. While archaeologists have discovered the bones of our oldest ancestors in just a few places, they have found many more remains in Africa from people who lived more than two million years ago—not only the peoples' bones, but also the remains of their food along with the world's oldest stone tools. Archaeologists have discovered that, from this time onward, people have grown in numbers and spread out to settle the rest of the world.

At first, our ancestors' ways of life changed very slowly, and their populations spread out only over Africa, Europe, and Asia. Many other changes also happened in our world during this time; it was the time of the great Ice Ages. The patterns of weather, the kinds of animals living in different places, and even the shape of the land itself all changed.

Over the many thousands of years of the Ice Ages, peoples' lives also changed. By 400,000 years ago, people had learned to use fire. By 100,000 years ago, they had learned to make very complicated tools out of stone, and some individuals had discovered and moved into Australia. By 40,000 years ago, wherever they lived, humans had become highly skilled gatherers and hunters of wild food, and excellent tool makers. They left remains of their campsites and tools, and sometimes their paintings and carvings, from western Europe and Africa across all of Asia and out to Australia.

Sometime during the final years of the last Ice Age, the first people arrived in the Americas. Since the American continents are surrounded by water, many theories have been proposed to explain how the first settlers reached this land. As you will read in Chapter 1, the archaeology of the Americas, known as "New World Archaeology," differs from that of Africa, Europe, and Asia. People have lived in the Old World for hundreds of thousands of years, but they have lived in the New World for perhaps only 12,000 years. Also, while some people in the Old World began writing as early as 5,000 years ago, few groups in the New World kept written records—or at least records that could be preserved—until after the Europeans arrived. As far as we know today, the only ancient New World people to keep many of their records in writing lived in Central America, where they began writing over 2,000 years ago. For all other peoples in the New World, written history began only when European explorers first reported what they saw. All the rest is open to us only through archaeology and the traditions of the surviving native peoples of the land.

This book is about the archaeology of one part of the New World, the part of North America that we now call the Northeast: New York, the six states of New England, and the southern Maritime Provinces of Canada. The first two chapters describe the last Ice Age in North America, the coming of the first Americans, and the ways of life of the very first peoples of the Northeast. The five chapters that follow describe what we know of the changes in peoples' ways of life in the Northeast up to the time of arrival of the first European settlers, and what happened with the arrival of the Europeans. A final chapter discusses the importance of archaeology and how you can help preserve knowledge of the past.

For those interested, there are also two Appendices. The first describes how archaeology works. It may help you better understand how archaeologists put together a picture of the past. The second tells you where to go to learn more about what archaeologists are doing, and how you can help save ancient remains in your own area. Of course, there is also a bibliography to help you find other books to read.

# 1

# The Ice Ages and the First Americans

The earth we live on is ever changing. The shapes of our hills and mountains, lakes and rivers, valleys and coastlines all constantly change. Sometimes they change very quickly, perhaps because of a flood, an earthquake, or the eruption of a volcano. Usually, though, they change too slowly for us to notice from one day to the next. Forces deep inside the earth can slowly push up mountains, open valleys, and even move the continents themselves, sometimes pushing them together and sometimes pulling them apart. At the same time, wind, rain, and snow; freezing and thawing; and the flow of the streams, currents, and ocean tides slowly wear the land down. We call this slow wearing-down of the land, "erosion."

The Northeast has not always looked the same as it does today. We have changed the shape of the land ourselves, of course, by clearing the forests, digging canals, leveling hills, and filling in wetlands. But nature has done much more, although much more slowly, over the past billion years. The outermost layer of the earth consists of many sections, called plates. These plates have been slowly, but constantly, moving. As they move, they press against each other, and this pressure sometimes forces the earth's surface to buckle, creating mountain ranges. In the area of the Northeast, such buckling formed the ancestors of the Taconic Mountains. Similar forces later produced the Appalachians, and, much later, the Adirondacks. Each time new mountains rose up, erosion began to wear them down, and the rocks and sand worn down from them slowly formed a wide "shelf" around the continents, under the ocean. Parts of these ancient mountains still exist today; we call them the Taconics, Green Mountains, Berkshires, White Mountains, Adirondacks, and Catskills.

Sometimes, too, the deep forces of our planet

pushed other continents up against our ancient continent, to build larger continents. Later, these same forces pulled the land apart again, leaving behind pieces of the many lands that had once been pushed together. Many parts of eastern New England and the Maritime Provinces of Canada contain pieces of other continents.

Today, there are no new mountain chains pushing up in our region. This has been a quiet land for at least two million years—but even a quiet land can change. During the past two million years, the greatest cause of change has been the coming and going of giant ice sheets. Scientists call the time of these ice sheets, the "Ice Ages." Nobody knows for certain what has caused the Ice Ages to begin or to end. The last great period of Ice Ages started about two million years ago and ended about 10,000 years ago. It is called the Pleistocene Epoch.

Heavy, thick sheets of ice, called glaciers, spread down from the northern polar ice cap and out from the higher mountains. Although the ice melted at its outer edges, more pushed down to replace it. The glaciers grew in much the same way as a puddle of water grows when you add more water, only much more slowly. As new snow fell on the glaciers each winter, its added weight pressed the older, lower layers into slush-like ice and forced the whole mass to spread out.

The glaciers caused enormous changes on the surface of the earth. They picked up huge boulders, gravel, and sand, and they carried them along over the landscape. This made the glaciers act like giant sheets of sandpaper. They scraped and gouged against mountains and down valleys, wearing down hills and grinding the stones in their path into a mixture of finer sands, gravels, and clays called "glacial drift." Eventually, the glaciers deposited this drift in

# Glaciers at their Farthest During the Last Ice Age

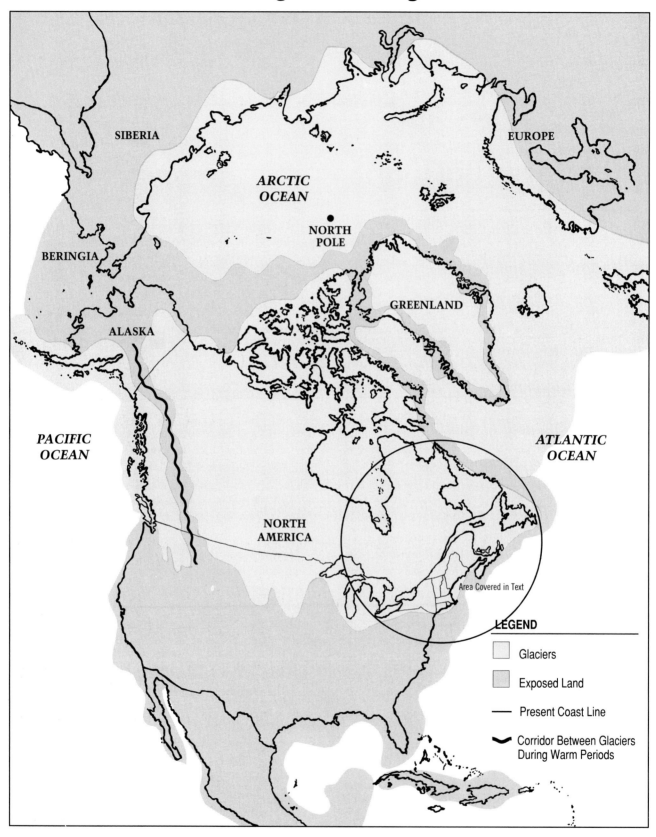

Figure 1: The northern ice cap, which today covers only the earth's northern polar region, extended much farther south during the Ice Ages. The ice sheets grew and shrank several times, often covering all of the Northeast as well as many other parts of the northern hemisphere. (After Canby, 1979, and Fladmark, 1986.)

# Typical Glacial Features of the Northeastern Landscape

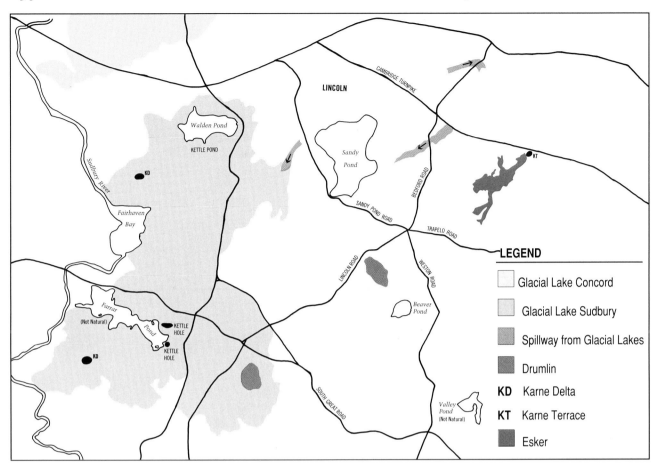

Figure 2: The area of Lincoln, Massachusetts, contains examples of almost every kind of deposit left by the glaciers, including kames, eskers, drumlins, drift, kettle holes, and the beds of large, temporary lakes. Glacial Lakes Concord and Sudbury formed when melting waters from the ice sheet to the north became trapped between the ice and the hills of Lincoln and the surrounding area. The lakes emptied only when the ice sheet shrank back further to the north, opening a passage for the water to the northeast—today's Concord River valley. (After Koteff, 1963 and 1964; Skehan, 1979.)

drumlins, moraines, eskers, and kames; and their melting waters spread the drift across many valleys. The melting waters also carved river valleys through the drift; but sometimes the waters became trapped between the ice sheet and higher ground, forming wide, temporary lakes. Sometimes, too, large blocks of ice fell off the melting edge of the ice and became buried in the drift. When these blocks melted, they left deep holes, called "kettle holes." These often filled with water, forming deep, permanent lakes.

The area once covered by the ice now contains many land-forms that were shaped by the moving or melting ice. Such places as Lake Champlain, Long Island, Cape Cod, the "notches" in the White Mountains of New Hampshire, the hills of Boston, the Sudbury and Concord River valleys, the Finger Lakes of New York, and the Hudson River valley all show the glaciers' handiwork. So, too, do many of the hills, streams, and ponds that became important to the first peoples of this land.

The weather changed many times during the Pleistocene Epoch. The glaciers grew out and then shrank back several times. Each time, it took the glaciers thousands of years to grow out and thousands more to shrink back again. When the ice sheets grew, the weather became colder. Between the Ice Ages came periods of warmer weather, during which the glaciers shrank and many areas became free of ice.

In the last Ice Age, beginning 60,000 to 70,000 years ago, two major ice sheets grew in North America (see Figure 1). One ice sheet spread out from western Canada, and one from eastern Canada. Most of the time, these two great glaciers lay far apart. During the coldest times, though, they grew so large that they

# Crossing the Bering Land Bridge

SIBERIA

ASIA

NORTH PACIFIC OCEAN

Figure 3: The joining together of Siberia and Alaska is very important in the history of North America, because it created land across which humans and other animals could migrate to the New World from Asia.

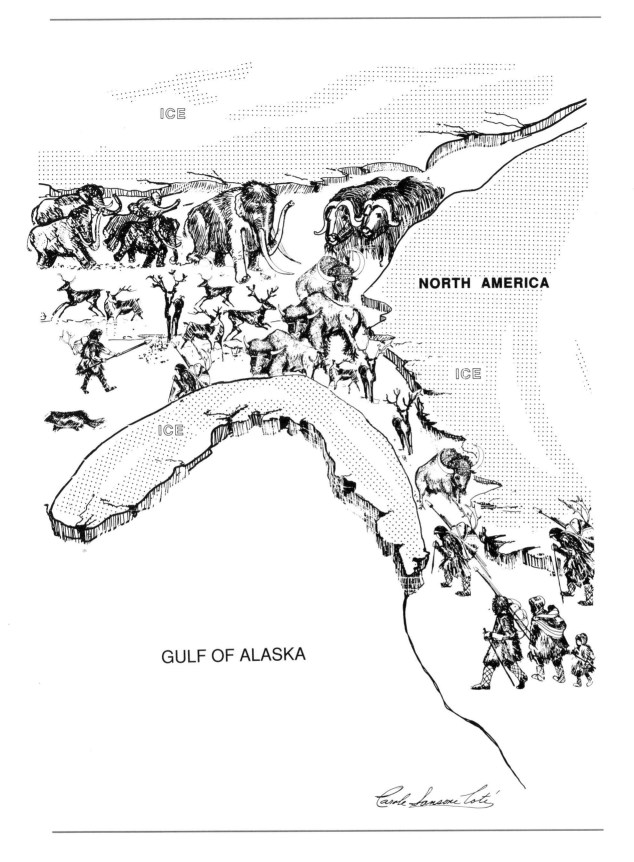

ICE

NORTH AMERICA

ICE

ICE

GULF OF ALASKA

joined together along a line just east of the Rocky Mountains. When they lay apart, a wide path or corridor of open land stretched from eastern Alaska all the way south to where Montana is now. The last very cold period was 18,000 years ago. The corridor stood open before then, and it opened again perhaps as early as 16,000 years ago.

The glaciers affected much more than just the shape of the land. The earth has a fixed amount of water. Some of this water flows in ponds, lakes, rivers, and oceans; some of it moves about in the atmosphere in clouds; and some of it lies frozen, mostly on high mountains and at the North and South Poles. Water constantly evaporates from the lakes and oceans to form clouds, and eventually it returns to earth as rain or snow. During the Ice Ages, much of the evaporated water returned to earth only as snow in the north. Less of this snow melted than fell each year. Much of the earth's supply of surface water thereby became locked up in the ice instead of flowing back to the oceans. As a result, the oceans of the world shrank and sea levels along the coasts fell. At times, the oceans lay as much as 100 to 150 meters (300 to 450 feet) below their present levels.

The oceans are often shallow around the edges of the continents. The bottom of the ocean in these shallow areas is called the "continental shelf." In some places, the continental shelf extends out several kilometers (or miles) under the ocean before it drops off into deep oceans. When the level of the world's oceans fell, their waters no longer covered the continental shelf. This gave the continents different shapes from those we know today (see Figure 1). Dry land existed where none had been before, and it became a home for many plants and animals.

One place where land emerged from the oceans lies between Siberia and Alaska, where the Bering Strait is today. The ocean level dropped so much that dry land reached all the way across between Siberia and Alaska, forming a passage or "land bridge" between Asia and North America (see Figure 3). Scientists call this ancient land bridge, "Beringia." At its greatest size, Beringia was 2,000 kilometers (about 1,200 miles) from north to south: as wide as one third the distance across the United States!

During the last Ice Age, most of Beringia, as well as most of northern Europe, Siberia, and the areas next to the glaciers in North America, was covered by tundra. This tundra consisted of cool, grass-covered plains, with scattered clumps of trees in sheltered parts of the valleys. By the beginning of this last Ice Age, people

lived all over Africa, Europe, and Asia. Those living in northern Europe and Asia had to find ways to survive in their tundra environment.

As they moved across the tundra, some people arrived in Alaska. Of course, they did not know that they were the first people ever to set foot in North America. Archaeologists have found evidence that, when the ice-free corridor opened between the two

vast ice sheets, some of these people ventured southward through Canada into what is now the northern United States. Some archaeologists are not sure that all of the first people to explore south of the ice sheets arrived by land—some people could have traveled down the sea coast, perhaps in boats. Other scientists see evidence that people arrived in North America even before the last Ice Age. Most archaeologists,

Figure 4: It may often have been cold, but the tundra was not a difficult place to live. The grasslands provided plant foods for humans, as well as food for herds of many large animals such as mammoths, reindeer, and musk ox, as well as for smaller animals such as deer, and for flocks of migratory birds. These animals in turn provided ample meat for the people who lived on the tundra, as well as furs for their clothing, and skins, bones, and sinew for making their tools. Some people even made their houses out of the skins, ribs, and other bones of the bigger animals they hunted.

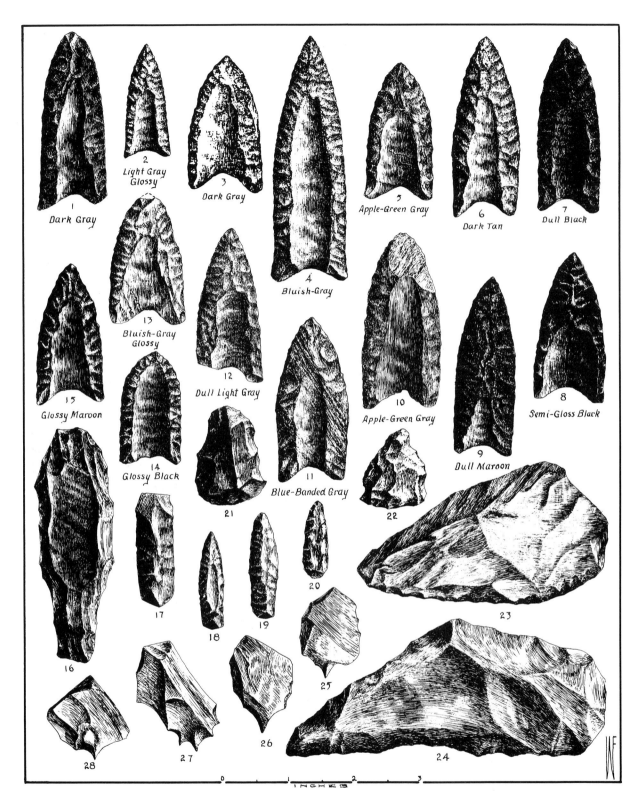

Figure 5: Archaeologists have found some of the tools used by the Paleo-Indians—the first people in the Americas—and their Siberian cousins. Most of these tools are made of stone. Wood-working tools made of stone show us that the Paleo-Indians may have used wooden tools, too, but these would have decayed a long time ago. By studying stone tools from a site, archaeologists can determine whether the site was left by Paleo-Indians, and they can learn about the craftsmanship and way of life of these people. (Numbers 1-15, fluted points; 16, side scraper; 17-20, drills; 21, 22, stem scrapers; 23, woodworking notcher; 24 Paleo knife [12.1 cm. (4.75 in.) long]; 25-28, gravers.) (Drawings by William Fowler for the Bulletin of the Massachusetts Archaeological Society, reproduced with permission.)

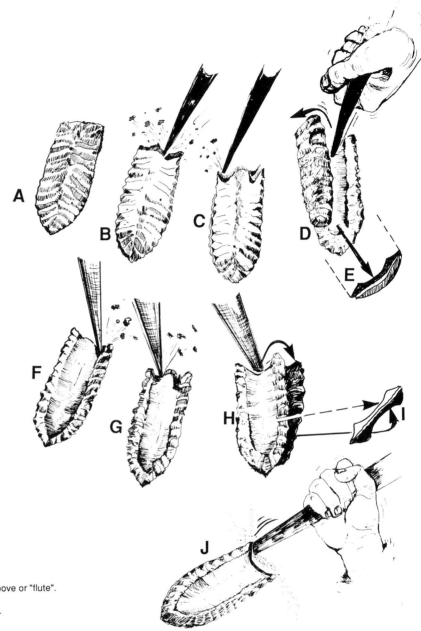

A. The point is roughed out to the general shape.

B. A notch is chipped in the base.

C. The notch is finished. A striking platform is left in the middle.

D. A sharp blow is hit against the striking platform and a long flake snaps out and creates a long groove or "flute".

E. Cross section of the point with the one fluted face.

F. A second basal notch is started on the other side.

G. The second notch is completed, creating a striking platform on the second side.

H. A sharp blow against the second striking platform removes the second long flake. Another fluted surface on the second side has been created.

I. Cross section of the point, showing the two fluted faces.

J. The base is ground to smooth it: the "ears" and edge have been reshaped by by fine chipping to sharpen the blade.

Figure 6: The Paleo-Indians made grooves, or flutes, in their spear points by removing a long, flat flake from the middle of each side, a very difficult and delicate job. The photograph shows a fluted point [4.3 cm. (1.75 in.) long] from Concord, Massachusetts. (Photograph from Blancke and Robinson, 1985, reproduced with the permission of the Concord Museum, Concord, Massachusetts.)

Figure 7: (a) We do not know exactly why the Paleo-Indians made flutes on their spear points. Perhaps the grooves helped them lash the point to the spear. (b) Hunters could have hurled their spears if the animal was at a close enough range. (c) For longer distances and greater power, the Paleo-Indians may have used an atlatl—a throwing stick that gave the hunter a longer reach. The hunters may have killed only one big animal at a time, sometimes first chasing it into the mud or over a cliff. (Figure 7b is a photograph of a painting in the Royal Ontario Museum, Toronto, reproduced with permission.)

though, believe the evidence points most clearly to a single path of arrival, through the ice-free corridor at the end of the last Ice Age.

To these people arriving in North America, the environment all along the regions near the glaciers was similar to what they had known in Siberia and Beringia. Once they found their way through the ice-free corridor, though, they found something very new indeed!

Near the glaciers, the new arrivals found the same tundra, with its similar plants, large wetlands, herd animals, and waterfowl. But south of the tundra was a whole new world. Nothing blocked the way for these people to spread, perhaps following the herd animals and the flocks of waterfowl, and spread out they did. Archaeologists call these first people to arrive in North America, "Paleo-Indians," meaning oldest or most ancient Indians.

The Paleo-Indians used a kind of stone that was particularly good for making tools. It was hard, but it could break into sharp, strong pieces. Skilled people could shape them into long, thin pieces, called flakes. The stone most often used for sharpening and flaking is called chert, which is like what is called flint in Europe. The finest chert is like very fine porcelain.

The Paleo-Indians made a distinctive kind of spear point—it is so distinctive that any time an archaeologist finds one someplace, he or she knows that a Paleo-Indian passed by there long ago. This kind of spear point is called a "fluted point." Fluted points are thin, narrow, leaf-shaped spear points made of chert (shown in Figures 5, 6, and 7). Indeed, unlike all other spear points of the Native Americans and their Siberian relatives, these points had long, flat grooves running straight up the middle of each side, from the base almost to the tip. Some archaeologists believe that, at the very first, the Paleo-Indians did not make fluted points, but the idea of fluting spread rapidly.

Fluted points were first found by amateur collectors in Clovis, New Mexico, and therefore are called Clovis points. Archaeologists have since also found Clovis and similar points all over North America. This may show that the invention of fluting spread rapidly among Paleo-Indians already living all over North America, or that Paleo-Indians spread rapidly across North America shortly after inventing fluting.

And some of these Paleo-Indians came to live in the Northeast.

# 2
# The Last Ice Age and the First People of the Northeast

In the Northeast, where New York, New England, Nova Scotia, and New Brunswick are now, the last ice sheet remained longer than it did in other parts of North America. It covered all the area until as late as 18,000 to 16,000 years ago. The last ice sheet destroyed all living things in its path.

In time, the great ice sheets finally began to melt, and the front edges of the ice gradually shrank back to the north. Most of the world's water was still frozen into great ice sheets, though, leaving the sea nearly 130 meters (400 feet) below where it is now. A vast stretch of land stood open on the continental shelf, from southern New York all the way up to Nova Scotia. Mammoths, mastodons, and other animals of the tundra thrived.

Much of today's Long Island, Martha's Vineyard, Nantucket, and Cape Cod did not exist before the ice sheets shrank north. Their landscapes formed mostly from the rocks and sands dropped by the melting ice. Georges Bank and the coasts of Rhode Island and Connecticut also formed from gravel left by the melting ice. Tundra covered the exposed lands. Much of the continental shelf still stood above water, but the oceans would rise over them again as the ice continued to melt.

The southern coastline of New England extended all the way to where Georges Bank is now, and Nova Scotia's coastline extended so far south that it almost touched the land at Georges Bank. These parts of the continental shelf that once stood above the ocean waters now lie beneath them, and they form a rich fishing area. In recent times, fishermen have caught mammoth and mastodon teeth while fishing off Georges Bank. Nobody has dredged up evidence of people, but the Bank lies over 100 meters below sea level today, so such evidence would be very difficult to find.

As the ice sheet retreated, many blocks of ice remained on the land, buried under glacial drift. These blocks gradually melted, leaving parts of the land

Figure 8 (Opposite): These maps of the Northeast show how the shape of the land changed as the ice sheet melted. (a) Between 18,000 and 16,000 years ago, ice covered most of the land. The weight of the ice pressed the earth down far below its present level. (b) By 15,000 years ago the ice sheet was beginning to recede. As the ice melted at the edge, moraines were deposited, to create the beginning of Long Island, Martha's Vineyard, Nantucket, and Cape Cod. (c) By 14,000 years ago the ice sheets had pulled back from the coast. The Lake Erie basin was filled by the water from the melting ice. The continental shelf stood open in some areas, but it was flooded by the rising sea in other areas. With the weight of the ice gone, though, all of the land slowly began to rise. (d) By 13,000 years ago, the ice sheet had pulled back still further, but it still blocked the Gulf of St. Lawrence. Huge lakes formed in some valleys; scientists have named the largest of these the Glacial Lakes Iroquois (A), Vermont (B), Albany (C), Hitchcock (D), and Upham (E). (e) Shortly after 12,000 years ago the ice sheet finally pulled back from the Gulf of St. Lawrence. Meltwater and sea water mixed and flooded the Gulf and turned Glacial Lake Vermont into a small inland sea, called the Champlain Sea (F). This sea teamed with fish and sea mammals. Without the waters from the melting ice sheet to keep them full, though, the other glacial lakes soon disappeared. With the weight of the ice gone, the lands around the Gulf began rising, and soon the sea waters no longer flooded the valley. Instead, fresh water from streams and rivers filled the valley, giving us the Lake Champlain we know today. (After Borns, 1985; Ritchie, 1980; Snow, 1980; and Teller, 1987.)

# Changes in the Northeastern Landscape as the Glaciers Receded

## a. 18,000 to 16,000 Years Ago

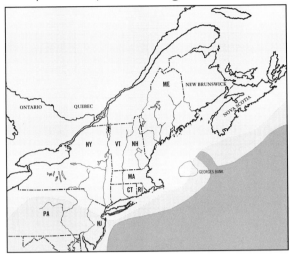

## b. By 15,000 Years Ago

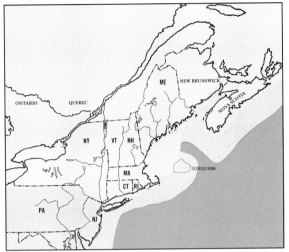

## c. By 14,000 Years Ago

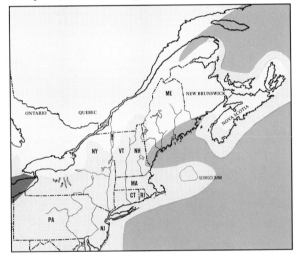

## d. By 13,000 Years Ago

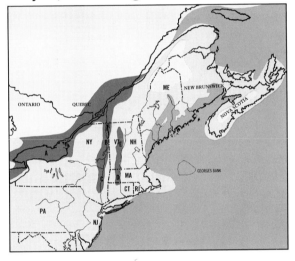

## e. By 12,000 Years Ago

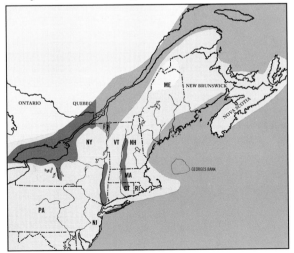

LEGEND

☐ Ice

☐ Exposed Land

☐ Sea Water

— Present Coastline

☐ Meltwater

HUNDREDS TO
THOUSAND
OF YEARS

**STEP 1**

PRESENT

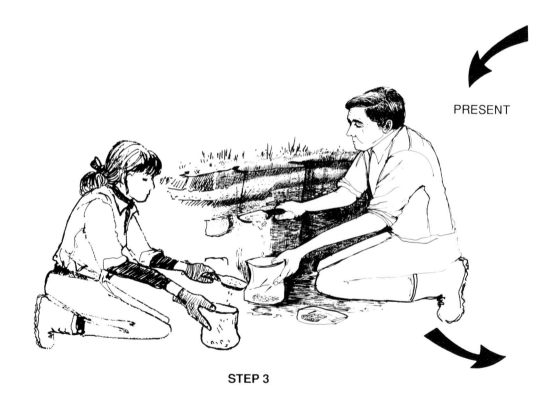

**STEP 3**

Figure 9: By studying ancient pollen, scientists learn when different plants returned to the Northeast. (1) Pollen from the trees and other plants often fell into the waters of the kettle ponds and bogs. (2) Layers of leaves and soil gradually filled in the ponds, and the surrounding forests grew. (3) Today, scientists remove the soil from the layers that have filled in a pond. (4) In the laboratory, the scientists use microscopes to see what kinds of pollen were preserved in the layers. (5) Finally, they put together a rough picture of how the region's plant life changed over time.

HUNDREDS TO
THOUSANDS
OF YEARS

STEP 2

STEP 4

# Some Paleo-Indian Sites

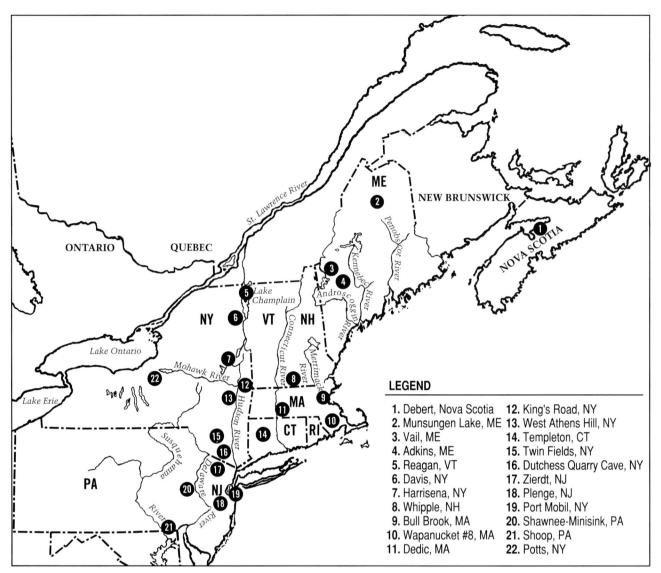

**LEGEND**

| | |
|---|---|
| 1. Debert, Nova Scotia | 12. King's Road, NY |
| 2. Munsungen Lake, ME | 13. West Athens Hill, NY |
| 3. Vail, ME | 14. Templeton, CT |
| 4. Adkins, ME | 15. Twin Fields, NY |
| 5. Reagan, VT | 16. Dutchess Quarry Cave, NY |
| 6. Davis, NY | 17. Zierdt, NJ |
| 7. Harrisena, NY | 18. Plenge, NJ |
| 8. Whipple, NH | 19. Port Mobil, NY |
| 9. Bull Brook, MA | 20. Shawnee-Minisink, PA |
| 10. Wapanucket #8, MA | 21. Shoop, PA |
| 11. Dedic, MA | 22. Potts, NY |

Figure 10: This map of the Northeast and surrounding regions shows the approximate locations of the earliest sites known to archaeologists, dating 10,000 to 11,000 years ago. The earliest visitors to the Hudson valley probably worked their way northward from the Susquehanna and Delaware River valleys. For a while, the huge glacial lakes and swollen rivers in the Hudson valley may have kept these people from moving further eastward. By 10,600 years ago, though, some of them had traveled as far north as Nova Scotia, where they left at least one large campsite, called Debert. (After Dincauze, 1979; Ritchie, 1980; Snow, 1980.)

dotted with kettle holes, some of which filled with the water and became kettle ponds. Cape Cod and Long Island have many of these round, deep kettle ponds. Walden Pond in Concord, Massachusetts, is a kettle pond made famous by Henry David Thoreau. Over the years, some kettle ponds have gradually filled with leaves and dirt, becoming bogs. These bogs are important for archaeology.

By 11,000 years ago, the melting glaciers filled the oceans still more, and sea waters began to cover the continental shelf. Southern New York and New England slowly began to shrink toward their present-day coastlines. The climate changed, too. The tundra and dry grasslands gradually changed into a warmer but still moist landscape of grassy plains with clumps of trees, especially in southern areas. Plants and animals driven away by the cold of the Pleistocene slowly returned.

Trees such as spruce, birch, jack pine, and red pine

returned first, as these plants can live better in cool, wet conditions than can others. Many of these kinds of trees still grow in the region. They are found in southern areas along the cool northern slopes of hills, while larger stands still grow in the north and in the mountains.

Unfortunately, we know less about the animals of the Northeast during the Pleistocene than we do about the plants. Animal bones do not preserve as well as pollen in our cold, wet region unless they happen to have fallen into a dry cave or a peat bog. For example, tusks and bones of a mastodon were found by chance in a bog in South Egremont, Massachusetts, in 1982. We can build a picture of the animal life in our region at the end of the Pleistocene by studying such rare finds, by using what we know about other parts of the continent, and by studying the descendants of Pleistocene animals still living on our continent today.

Evidence shows that the open tundra and grasslands changed into groves of pine, spruce, hemlock, and shrubs, especially in the southern parts of our region. Animals that preferred the cooler climate and vegetation near the ice sheet moved northward or else died out. In their place came animals such as caribou and others that preferred the new mixture of grasses, shrubs, and woodlands. Wetlands around the lakes in the Connecticut and Hudson valleys probably also attracted many waterfowl during the warmer times of the year.

The first humans arrived only slowly onto this stage. We know of few sites where Paleo-Indian people stayed for very long or in large numbers. Sometimes, all we find are one or two tools lying on the ground where someone dropped them long ago. We can guess that there probably were not many people in the Northeast at any one time during the Paleo-Indian period—perhaps only a few hundred. We also can guess that these people lived in small groups and traveled often, following the seasonal movements of their game. After so many hundreds of centuries, of course, many Paleo-Indian sites may have disappeared through erosion, and through unintentional destruction by modern society. (Chapter 8 tells you how you can help rescue sites from any more destruction.)

With so few sites to study, we know much less about the Paleo-Indians than we do about the later inhabitants of our region. However, we can study people who still lived by gathering and hunting in modern times elsewhere in the world. Such studies help us make sense of the few Paleo-Indian sites found. We can form a hypothesis: an idea that guides us in seeking out new evidence or in studying the evidence already excavated.

Archaeologists have learned that it is not easy to live by gathering plants and small animals and by hunting migratory animals for food, especially in a cold land. Each band of Paleo-Indians needed to know its territory very well—where each kind of plant or animal could be found at different times of the year, where the herds would pass as they migrated, where the best places were for watching for game or surprising it, where the best places were to get chert for the tools, and many more things. The people also needed to share what they knew with each other, to help each other get by. The people of each band also probably kept to a single territory, where they could put their knowledge and sharing to best use. When you think of these earliest people, you should think of them as moving in a regular pattern over a land they knew well, not wandering aimlessly.

Archaeologists have not yet found evidence of the shelters used by Paleo-Indians in the Northeast—not even a posthole. Postholes are stains left in the ground after the posts of a shelter have been taken out or left to rot. The holes that once held the posts become filled in with soils that have a different color than the surrounding ground. An archaeologist can tell where posts once stood by looking for their filled-in holes.

We know nothing about the religious beliefs of the Paleo-Indians. No burials of these people have been found in the Northeast, and only a few in the whole continent. People who live by gathering and hunting usually bury their dead wherever they happen to be when the death occurs. They surely knew many things and had many ideas about their world, but we may never discover them.

The first people of the Northeast used tools similar to those used by Paleo-Indians all over North America. Every band probably swapped news and ideas with its neighbors, and they all lived in the same tundra environment, so it makes sense that they made their tools in similar ways. Yet even though they used the same kinds of tools, the Paleo-Indians in different parts of the Northeast made these tools in slightly different ways. Archaeologists have discovered at least seven slightly different shapes of spear points, but they are not sure what these differences tell us. Perhaps seven distinct bands of Paleo-Indians lived in the Northeast, making their spear points in similar but slightly different ways.

Like the Paleo-Indians elsewhere in North America,

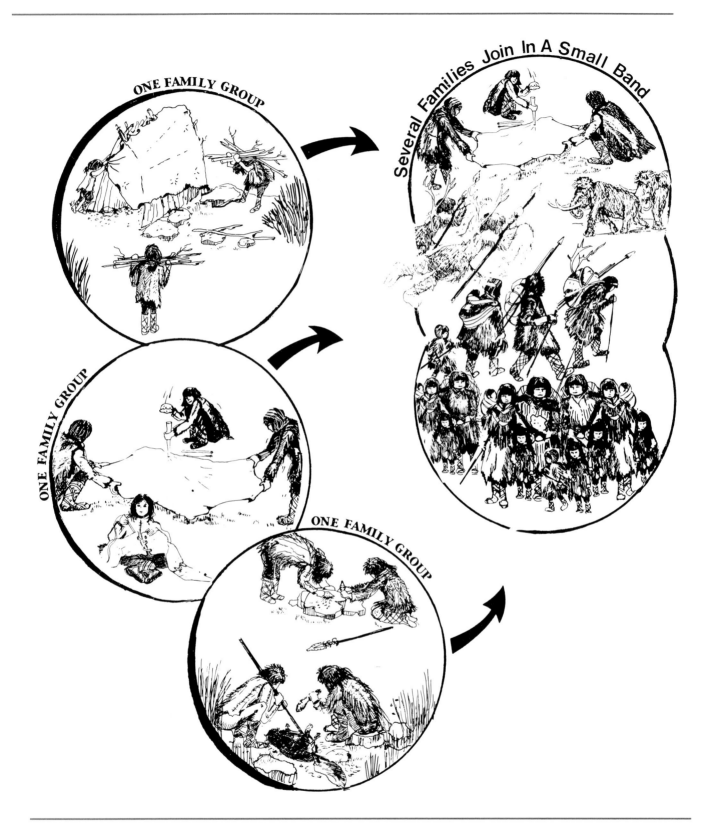

ONE FAMILY GROUP

ONE FAMILY GROUP

ONE FAMILY GROUP

Several Families Join In A Small Band

Figure 11: Archaeologists think that the earliest people of the Northeast lived in bands of closely related families. These bands would have traveled to find the plants and animals on which they depended for food, clothing, shelter, and tools. Sometimes in-dividuals or small teams may have gone off to gather or hunt their foods separately; sometimes single families may have traveled alone; and sometimes the entire band would have worked together.

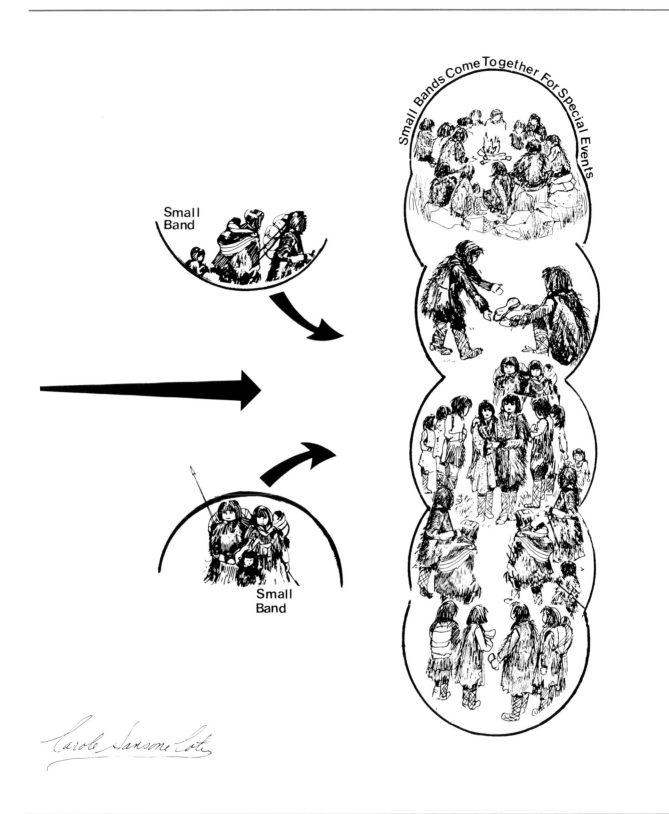

Small Band

Small Bands Come Together For Special Events

Small Band

Carole Sansone Coti

Figure 12: The Paleo-Indians probably made shelters similar to ones used by other hunting peoples who lived by traveling over cold lands. These shelters would have been simple windbreaks, made of brush with animal skins thrown over their tops and sides, each large enough for only a single family. This picture shows what archaeologists think one shelter looked like, at the Adkins Site in Maine. (Drawing by William Parsons for Richard M. Gramly, reproduced with permission.)

Summer

Spring

Fall

Winter

Figure 13: Many of the animals living in the Northeast during the Paleo-Indian period would have migrated every year from north to south and then back north again, in a cycle, as their plant foods ripened in different places. The earliest people of the Northeast prob- ably followed this same cycle, dining on many kinds of plants as well as on mastodon, caribou, moose, giant beavers, musk-ox, waterfowl, small mammals, and fish.

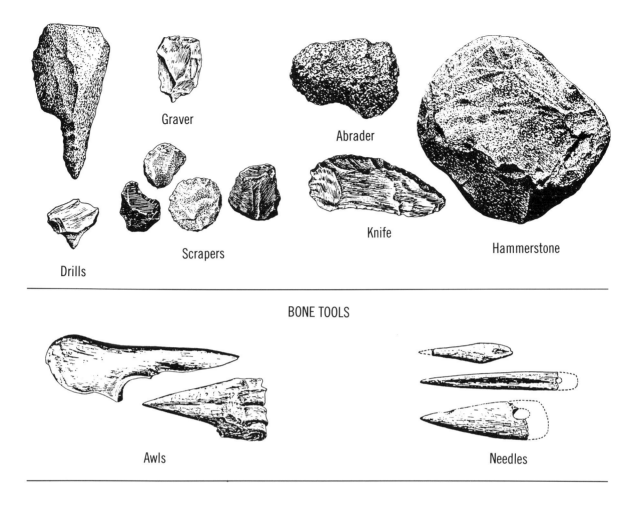

Graver

Abrader

Drills

Scrapers

Knife

Hammerstone

BONE TOOLS

Awls

Needles

Figure 14: The earliest people of the Northeast used stone tools called awls, drills, perforators, gravers, spokeshaves, and abraders to make useful items from wood and bone. They used stone scrapers and knives, and bone awls and needles to make useful items from animal hides and plant fibers. They also used the knives to butcher meat; and they used choppers and hammerstones to chop wood, break bones, pound plant foods, and make their finer stone tools. (Drawings by William Fowler for the Bulletin of the Massachusetts Archaeological Society, reproduced with permission.)

those who lived in the Northeast surely made tools from many materials, but only the tools made of stone have been preserved. Some of the stone they used came from quarries far away from the sites where the tools were buried. This may tell us that people of different bands traded with each other for some of their materials. Even though archaeologists have found no Paleo-Indian tools made of animal skins, plant fibers, bone, or wood, they have found stone tools shaped for working on these materials. These special stone tools usually are found at larger sites, where entire bands must have camped as a group. From this, we can guess that the people made most of their tools while staying at their main camps, although sometimes they may have had to fix a tool or make a temporary one while out gathering plants, hunting, or fishing.

Archaeologists in the Northeast have found only a few Paleo-Indian sites in caves or on valley floors. Instead, most sites are on the sides of valleys, or where the shores of glacial lakes once stood, or on hilltops that once overlooked grasslands. Such hilltops would have been dry places to live during those moist times, and sometimes they would have been places from which to watch migrating herds in the surrounding land. Some settlers also may have lived on the lands of the continental shelf, but those lands now lie under the ocean, and the sea may have washed their sites away or buried them beyond our reach.

The Paleo-Indian period began in the Northeast

Figure 15: This photograph of a diorama in the New York State Museum presents a picture of life at West Athens Hill, a Paleo-Indian campsite. It was developed by archaeologists and artists working together. (Photograph courtesy of the New York State Museum.)

before 11,000 years ago. It lasted until around 10,000 years ago, when there was an abrupt change in the kinds of tools the people made. The changing climate by this time had altered the region's vegetation and animal life; some of the larger animals of the last Ice Age became extinct. It seems likely that the people living in the Northeast adjusted by changing their tools, their patterns of travel, and their ways of gathering and hunting for food. It is possible that some Paleo-Indian bands died out or moved away. However, it seems that others stayed, survived, and changed their ways of life. They began a new stage of the region's history, called the Archaic period.

# 3

# The Early and Middle Archaic Periods

The migratory herds of large, Ice-Age animals gradually disappeared from the Northeast. By 10,000 years ago (8,000 B.C.), they were gone. The climate warmed and the edge of the ice sheet retreated far into Canada. Indeed, the environment would continue to change long after the glaciers departed. By 4,000 to 3,000 B.C., the climate may even have been warmer than today. As the climate warmed, plants and animals that could not stand the cold weather of the Pleistocene slowly spread into the Northeast, and forests gradually covered the land.

As the land changed, the people of our region adjusted their ways of life. Some people may even have left the region. In fact, many portions of the Northeast appear to be empty of sites dating between 8,000 and 6,000 B.C. Other people did stay, however, and their numbers slowly grew. They found new ways to feed and clothe themselves. They gathered many more nuts, berries, and roots from plants newly spreading into the region. They found different animals to hunt and new ways to bring in fish. We call this period of new ways of life, between 8,000 and 1,000 B.C., the Archaic. Archaeologists divide the Archaic period into three parts: the "Early Archaic," from 10,000 to 8,000 years ago (8,000 to 6,000 B.C.); the "Middle Archaic," from 8,000 to 6,000 years ago (6,000 to 4,000 B.C.); and the "Late Archaic," from 6,000 to 3,000 years ago (4,000 to 1,000 B.C.). This chapter looks at changes that took place during the Early and Middle Archaic; Chapter 4 looks at the even greater changes that took place during the Late Archaic alone.

## The Early Archaic Period

We can begin to understand what happened during the Archaic by going back to its beginnings, to the end of the Pleistocene, 10,000 years ago. Spruce, pine, and hemlock forests gradually replaced the tundra grasses across the northern parts of the land. This was still a cold land. But in the south, along the coast and the larger river valleys, the land was warmer and more comfortable for people and for many plants and animals. At first, spruce and pine trees spread out to replace the tundra, but soon oaks moved in to become the most numerous trees of all.

Waters from the melting glaciers continued to fill the oceans, but so slowly that, for a while, parts of the continental shelf still stayed dry. Along the shores, the ocean also held many more fish and sea mammals. Especially abundant were fish that leave the ocean each spring and migrate up freshwater streams to spawn. These fish were important food resources for people living or traveling along the coasts. Yet, they could be caught in the streams only at certain times of the year and only in certain places. The most important of these migrating fish were the Atlantic salmon, alewives, and shad.

The places where rivers and streams meet the ocean are called "estuaries." Estuaries are rich habitats for birds, fish, shellfish, and many other animals, including people. Some Archaic people probably lived along the shores of the land's many estuaries. However, the rising sea level flooded many of these

# Some Early and Middle Archaic Sites

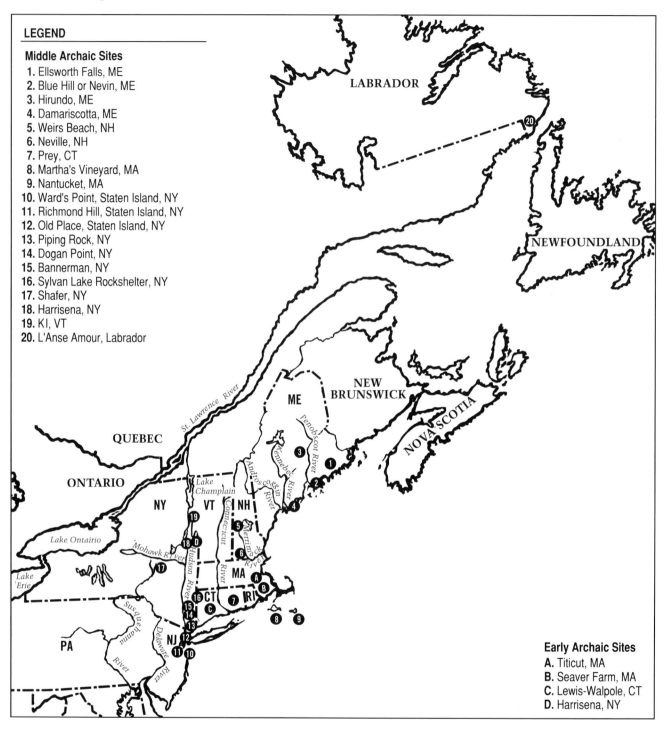

**LEGEND**

**Middle Archaic Sites**
1. Ellsworth Falls, ME
2. Blue Hill or Nevin, ME
3. Hirundo, ME
4. Damariscotta, ME
5. Weirs Beach, NH
6. Neville, NH
7. Prey, CT
8. Martha's Vineyard, MA
9. Nantucket, MA
10. Ward's Point, Staten Island, NY
11. Richmond Hill, Staten Island, NY
12. Old Place, Staten Island, NY
13. Piping Rock, NY
14. Dogan Point, NY
15. Bannerman, NY
16. Sylvan Lake Rockshelter, NY
17. Shafer, NY
18. Harrisena, NY
19. KI, VT
20. L'Anse Amour, Labrador

**Early Archaic Sites**
A. Titicut, MA
B. Seaver Farm, MA
C. Lewis-Walpole, CT
D. Harrisena, NY

Figure 16: This map of the Northeast and surrounding regions shows the approximate locations of Early and Middle Archaic sites known to archaeologists. Notice how few Early Archaic sites there are, and how many more sites there are from the Middle Archaic than from the Early Archaic. (After Dincauze, 1979; Ritchie, 1980; Snow, 1980; Tuck, 1976.)

# Food Animals in the Northeast Around 8000 BC

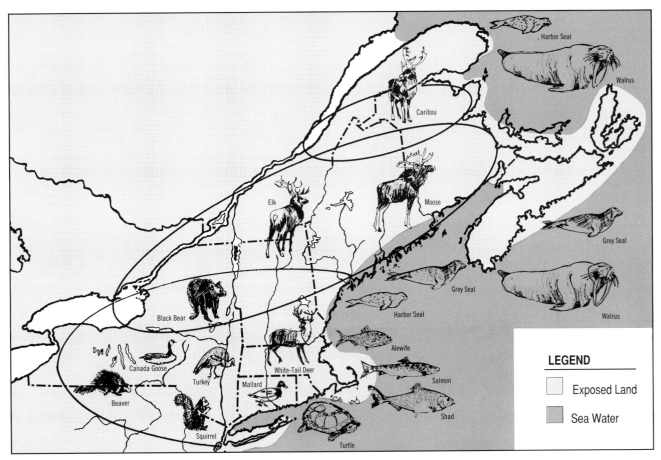

Figure 17: The Early Archaic people of the Northeast, around 8,000 B.C., hunted more animals of the forests and fewer animals of the open grasslands than had their Paleo-Indian ancestors.

ancient estuaries, destroying some while creating others. As the ocean waters rose, too, they probably destroyed shoreline sites dating from the Archaic period, just as they surely destroyed sites of the Paleo-Indians. Indeed, sea levels continued to rise steadily until late in the Archaic period, and, although much more slowly, they may still be rising even today.

Archaeologists have found only a few remains from the Early Archaic period in the Northeast. Indeed, there are fewer sites known from the Early Archaic than from the Paleo-Indian period. Why should this be? Most Early Archaic sites are in the southern and coastal areas, and there are no large hilltop sites, such as the Paleo-Indians once used. Archaeologists suspect that there simply were no longer any migrating herds to watch, but it also seems likely that there were just fewer people living in the Northeast, especially in the north. As is often the case, archaeologists have no simple explanations for the evidence they turn up.

Often, sites from the Early Archaic contain only one or two items—perhaps one or two tools or flakes of stone. This tells us something about the way of life at this time. Unlike the Paleo-Indians, the Early Archaic people must have traveled widely in very small groups for most of every year. They did not camp together in larger bands as often as their Paleo-Indian forebears, and so they left fewer sites with large numbers of tools and other remains.

Early Archaic people probably gathered many kinds of roots, nuts, and berries, and they also probably ate many small land animals, such as squirrels and beaver. Herds of large game no longer moved across the land, and deer probably became the principal large-game animal. Moose, bear, and a few caribou still living in the new forests also could have provided food. Even at sites near rivers and lakes, though, archaeologists have not yet found evidence that these people did much fishing—either in the form of fishing tools or the remains of the fish themselves.

Figure 18: Archaeologists have found only one large site from Early Archaic times in the Northeast. The Titicut site near the Taunton River in Massachusetts was a base camp for several families who probably hunted and collected all over southeastern New England. Excavations at this and other, smaller sites have helped archaeologists put together a limited picture of life at an Early Archaic base camp. (Photograph of a diorama at the former Bronson Museum, Attleboro, Massachusetts, by John Seakwood for the Massachusetts Archaeological Society, reproduced with permission of the photographer and the Society. The diorama will be reconstructed at the Robbins Museum, Middleboro, Massachusetts.)

Gathering roots, nuts, and berries takes only a few people at any one time. And most of the time, one or two hunters working together could have hunted more easily than could a larger group, particularly when hunting deer. Deer do not migrate. They spread out in the woods year-round, coming together in herds only when it is very cold or at their time of mating. Indeed, all of the animals eaten in the Early Archaic were best hunted or trapped by only one or two people at a time.

Small groups traveling by themselves and living by gathering and hunting would rarely leave archaeological sites behind them that we might be able to find and recognize easily today, not even at their temporary camps. Early Archaic people would have returned often only to certain kinds of places: perhaps large stands of oak trees that produced good quantities of acorns; streams where fish migrated; wetlands where migratory birds came to rest on their yearly journeys; or sheltered spots along a river or lake in a good hunting area. Only a few of these places would have provided enough food for families to camp together and enjoy each other's company. Archaeologists call this rare kind of camp, a "base camp."

We can as yet say very little about social life during the Early Archaic period. The people surely had to stay in touch to help each other, to find mates, to consult with elders for advice, or to learn about new methods for making tools. They also probably shared information on good spots to collect plants and other materials, or to hunt or fish. The Early Archaic stone tools found from eastern Massachusetts to the Hudson River and beyond all have the same shapes, but they are almost always made out of local kinds of stone. This tells us that people stayed in touch but did not trade much with each other across any great distances—at least not for the stone they used in their tools. More than this we cannot yet say. We know much more about the people of later times.

## The Middle Archaic Period

The Middle Archaic period, from 8,000 to 6,000 years ago (6,000 to 4,000 B.C.), was a time of many changes.

The ocean during Middle Archaic times still stood as much as 9 meters (29 feet) lower than it is today, but it rose steadily. Along the seashore, the estuaries grew and shifted with the rising ocean waters. Large tidal flats, although common today, probably did not yet exist. The ocean currents running along the shore shifted as the ocean waters rose, changing the shape of the coast. Some parts of the continental shelf still stood above the ocean waters and this land undoubtedly attracted both game animals and people. Inland, the rivers and streams finished carving their valleys into the shapes we see today.

In this changing land, the Middle Archaic people of the Northeast learned new ways to catch fish along the estuaries, rivers, and streams. And their ways of hunting in the forests also became more complicated. Archaeologists have found sites near lakes, bogs, marshes, and meadows; of course, many of the bogs, marshes, and meadows of today were still lakes back then. These would have been good places to hunt for migrating birds, as well as turtles, frogs, snakes, fish, and small mammals. The people also gathered more kinds and quantities of nuts and probably many other plant materials than ever before. In the north, especially, people along the coasts also began hunting and fishing out on the open ocean.

The people who lived in the southern parts of our region began returning to the same camping spots year after year. They even used some sites over and over again for hundreds of years. Archaeologists have found many more sites from this period than from the Early

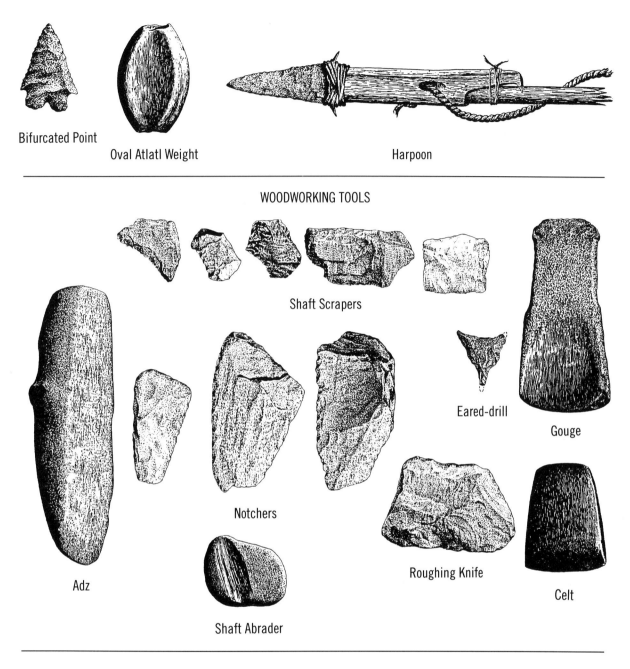

HUNTING TOOLS

Bifurcated Point

Oval Atlatl Weight

Harpoon

WOODWORKING TOOLS

Shaft Scrapers

Eared-drill

Gouge

Adz

Notchers

Shaft Abrader

Roughing Knife

Celt

Archaic, and these sites often have larger rubbish dumps than before. (The map in Figure 16 gives you some idea of how many more sites have been found.) The number of people must have begun to increase, perhaps because the climate had improved and food-plants and animals had become more abundant. Perhaps, too, as daily chores grew and changed, parents found some benefit in having larger families to help out.

Figure 19: Archaeologists have found many kinds of stone tools at sites dating from the Early Archaic period. Many of these tools were used for carving wood and bone, so we can guess that the people also made other tools of wood, bone and antler, animal hides, and plant fibers. Unfortunately, none of these other tools has been preserved. For example, the people probably also used wooden sticks to dig for tubers and roots. Early Archaic hunters used a different kind of spear point than did the Paleo-Indians. When archaeologists find this distinctive point at a site, they know that someone camped there between 10,000 and 8,000 years ago (8,000 to 6,000 B.C). (Drawings by William Fowler for the Bulletin of the Massachusetts Archaeological Society, reproduced with permission.)

## Life in the Middle Archaic in the Southern Areas

**Summer**

**Small Coastal Camp Shellfishing**

**Fall**

**Small Camp**

**Catching migrating birds**

**Small Camp**

Figure 20: The Middle Archaic people of southern New York and New England most likely followed a regular cycle of gathering and hunting in different places through each year. The sites we have found show us that they often returned to the same places year after year, following the cycle of the seasons.

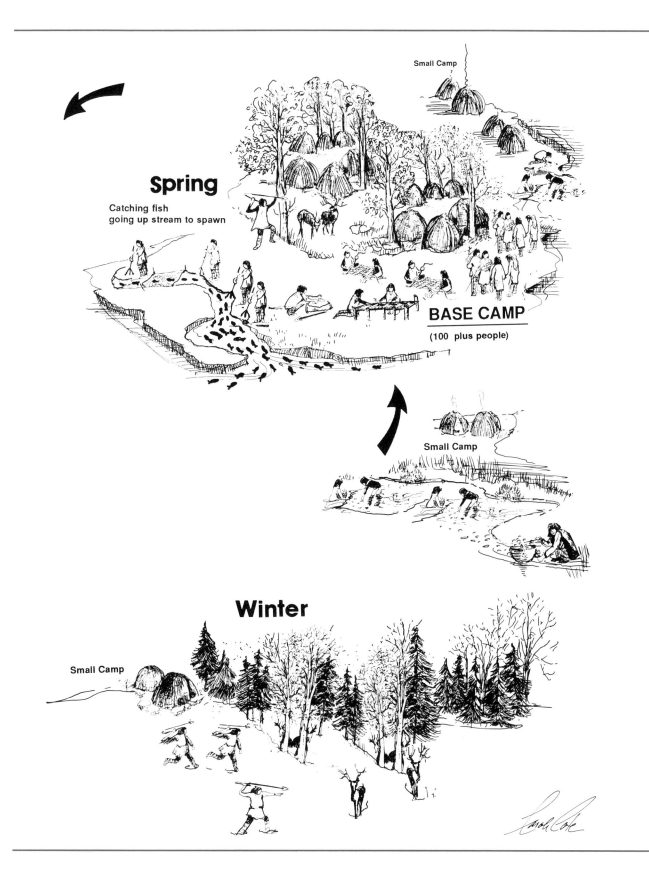

**Spring**

Catching fish
going up stream to spawn

Small Camp

**BASE CAMP**

(100 plus people)

Small Camp

Small Camp

**Winter**

Figure 21: The Neville site in New Hampshire had three major Archaic levels. All three levels, but especially the lowest (earliest) level, contained evidence of a great many fish, which indicates that the site was an active fishing camp during the entire period. The excavations uncovered different kinds of stone tools in each level, along with animal bones and charcoal. The kinds of stone tools show us that three different groups of people lived at Neville, one after the other. All together, these people used the site for over 2,500 years. There were few hide-working or plant-processing tools in the lowest level. Since hides are not good in the spring and young plants do not need processing, archaeologists believe that the earliest level was used only in the spring. At the middle Archaic level, the presence of woodworking, hunting, and hide-working tools suggests that people camped at Neville in those years during the summer and fall. There were fewer tools in the highest Archaic level, which might indicate that it was only a small, temporary hunting and fishing camp during that period. (Drawings by William Fowler for the Bulletin of the Massachusetts Archaeological Society, reproduced with permission.)

HIGHEST LEVEL     4000 B.C.

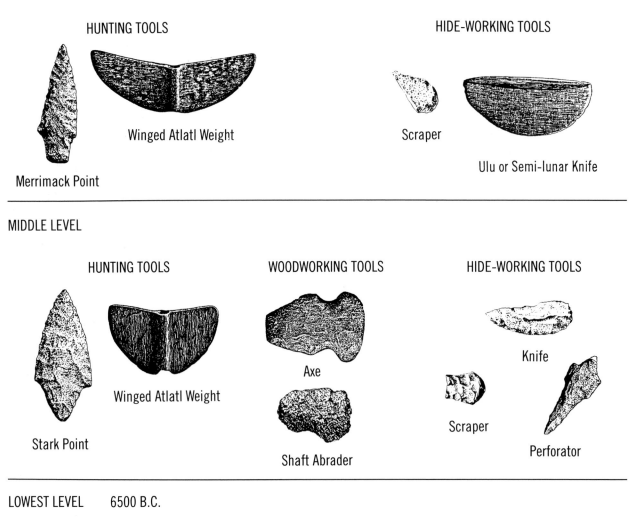

HUNTING TOOLS

Winged Atlatl Weight

Merrimack Point

HIDE-WORKING TOOLS

Scraper

Ulu or Semi-lunar Knife

MIDDLE LEVEL

HUNTING TOOLS

Winged Atlatl Weight

Stark Point

WOODWORKING TOOLS

Axe

Shaft Abrader

HIDE-WORKING TOOLS

Knife

Scraper

Perforator

LOWEST LEVEL     6500 B.C.

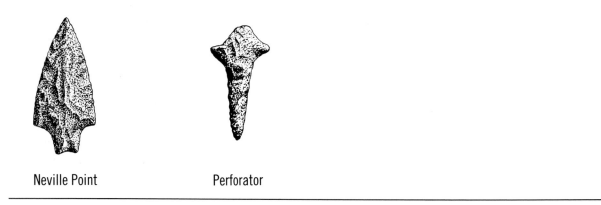

Neville Point

Perforator

Figure 22: From the excavations at Neville and other sites, archaeologists and artists have put together a scene showing Middle Archaic fishing methods. (Photograph from the University of New Hampshire Media Center, Durham, New Hampshire, reproduced with permission.)

The Neville site is one of the best known Middle Archaic excavations in the entire eastern United States. It overlooks Amoskeag Falls on the Merrimack River in Manchester, New Hampshire. The site was destroyed by construction work in 1968, but not before amateur archaeologists had a chance to rescue much information about how people lived in the southern parts of the Northeast during this period.

By Middle Archaic times, the river at the Neville site had much the same shape as it has today. There also were many small lakes and streams in the area. Each year, fish swam up the river on their way to spawn in the quiet lakes and ponds beyond. The Falls were an ideal place to catch fish, and people gathered there year after year, for hundreds of years, to bring in as many fish as they could.

Along with fish, birds, mammals, and plant foods, some Middle Archaic people in the southern parts of our region also ate shellfish. We know this because

they left behind heaps of shells. Although archaeologists have found only a few Middle Archaic shell heaps, mostly in the Hudson valley, other heaps probably washed away as the ocean rose over the older coastlines (see Figure 23). Some Middle Archaic shell heaps were quite large, but the people probably never counted on clams or oysters for most of their food. There is more meat in a single deer than in a thousand clams or oysters.

The people living in the northern parts of our region during the Middle Archaic period also developed a new way of life, but one quite different from that of their southern neighbors. The people of the northern lands began returning to favored spots year after year, and they, too, left an increasing number of sites. (The map in Figure 16 gives you an idea of how many more sites have been found in this part of our region.)

Middle Archaic people who came to live along the northern coasts found that the shores grew particularly rich each spring and fall with migrating herds of sea mammals. Later, as they learned to take further advantage of this rich opportunity for hunting, the Late Archaic descendants of these people eventually de-

# Changing Forests in the Archaic Period

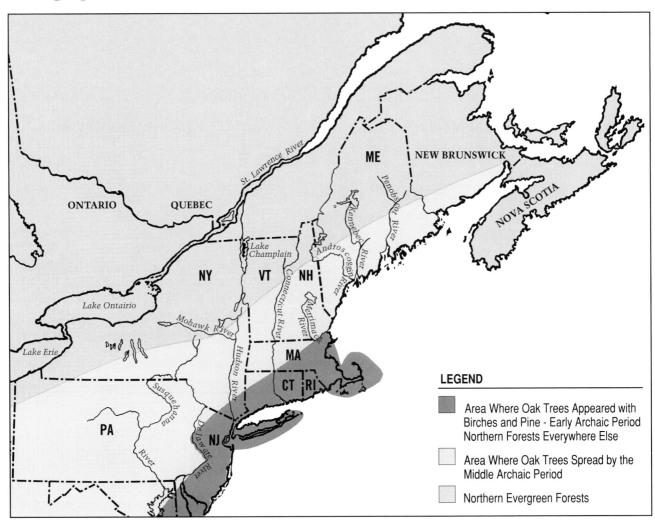

**LEGEND**

▉ Area Where Oak Trees Appeared with Birches and Pine - Early Archaic Period Northern Forests Everywhere Else

☐ Area Where Oak Trees Spread by the Middle Archaic Period

☐ Northern Evergreen Forests

Figure 23: By studying pollen, scientists have discovered that oak trees began to grow again in the southern lands of the Northeast sometime during the Early Archaic period. By the end of the Middle Archaic period, the forests all across the Northeast had come to resemble closely the way they would be just before the coming of the first Europeans. As the climate changed, so, too, did the shape of the land. The glaciers continued to melt far to the north, and the ocean waters continued to rise. The coastlines of Long Island and Cape Cod began to emerge by around 7,000 B.C., but Martha's Vineyard and Nantucket were then still part of the mainland. (After Borns, 1985; Snow, 1980.)

veloped a special and unique way of life, called the "Maritime Archaic."

Our best evidence of life during the Middle Archaic in the northern Northeast comes from a site called L'Anse Amour, in Labrador. There, archaeologists have discovered the oldest burial mound in the world, built about 7,500 years ago. On each side of the burial were signs of a fire. Among the pieces of charcoal from the fires were pieces of burned bones of mammals and birds. The people at L'Anse Amour placed many objects alongside their dead. Perhaps they believed in an afterlife, where the dead could use the objects left with them in their graves. The objects included stone and bone points and knives. The most important discovery was a walrus tusk and an unusual antler harpoon tip called a "toggling harpoon" point. The harpoon point probably once was attached to a harpoon shaft with a hide line. When the harpoon was speared into a fish or sea mammal and the shaft pulled back, the point would twist around and become caught in the wound; the hunter could then pull the animal back to shore. Archaeologists believe that this is the oldest toggling harpoon point ever found. It shows how advanced the people of L'Anse Amour were in sea hunting.

Figure 24: Middle Archaic tools from the site of L'Anse Amour in Labrador included a simple whistle. (Photograph courtesy of the New York State Museum.)

The Middle Archaic period was one of great changes. By the end of this period, the people in every part of our region were beginning to shape ways of life that fit their own particular areas and climates. The story of the next period, the Late Archaic, is the story of the people who gave full shape to these many new and different ways of life.

# 4

# The Late Archaic Period

Archaeologists have found many sites from the Late Archaic period, 6,000 to 3,000 years ago (4,000 to 1,000 B.C.), all over the Northeast. We have a lot of information, but archaeologists are not as yet sure what it all tells us. One thing we do know for sure, though, is that more people lived in our region than ever before.

The Late Archaic people who lived in different parts of the Northeast developed different ways of life, tied closely to the plants, animals, and climate of each part of the region. Along the far northeastern coasts, the people developed a way of life closely tied to the sea. Archaeologists now call this way of life the "Maritime" Archaic. To the west, in Vermont and New York, the people developed a way of life tied to the interior forests, rivers, and lakes called the "Lake Forest" or "Laurentian" Archaic. To the south, the slightly warmer forests, rivers, and lakes allowed the people to develop yet other ways of life. Some southern people lived along the coast, taking much of their food from the region's rich estuaries, shoreline, and ocean; others lived along the rivers and lakes of the southern interior forests. Archaeologists call these more southern ways of life by several names, most often the "Atlantic Seaboard" or sometimes the "Mast Forest" Archaic ("mast forest" refers to a forest of nut-bearing trees).

The people following these different ways of life shared their knowledge of new tools and ideas with each other. They probably lived similar daily lives, but with important and very interesting differences. We will look at each of these in turn, to see both how similar and different they were.

## The Maritime Archaic

Forests of birches and evergreens covered the northern lands of the Maritime Archaic people. The land provided many plant foods, and many animals lived in the forests, such as caribou, moose, and black bear, as well as beaver, foxes, and smaller mammals. But the ocean was the greatest source of food, and probably of many other materials used in daily life.

Archaeologists have learned a lot about the people of the Maritime Archaic, mostly from their burials. The burials all have one striking feature. The bodies were all covered with a red powder called ocher, making everything look as though it was painted red. For a long time, archaeologists called these people the "Red Paint People."

The people who left behind the Red Paint cemeteries lived in Maine and in the Maritime Provinces of Canada. These people placed many tools and ornaments in the graves of their dead. Often the bones of the dead have long since crumbled away, but a cemetery excavated at the site of Port Au Choix, Newfoundland, is an important exception. Here, shells and sand covered the bones and helped to preserve them.

The cemetery at Port Au Choix contained the skeletons of 100 people of all ages and of both sexes. The people were healthy and strong. Their teeth showed heavy wear—probably from chewing animal hides to make the hides soft—but they had no cavities. The people of Port Au Choix probably lived in different places at different times of the year, going wherever they could most easily catch their foods. Year after year, however, they came back to Port Au Choix to fish and to hunt the sea mammals that migrated past in the spring and fall.

Cemeteries like the one at Port Au Choix have been found down the coast as far south as the Androscoggin River valley in Maine. The cemeteries in Maine contain many heavy tools made of slate. These were probably used for shaping large objects out of wood. Archaeologists began studying these sacred

# Some Late Archaic Sites

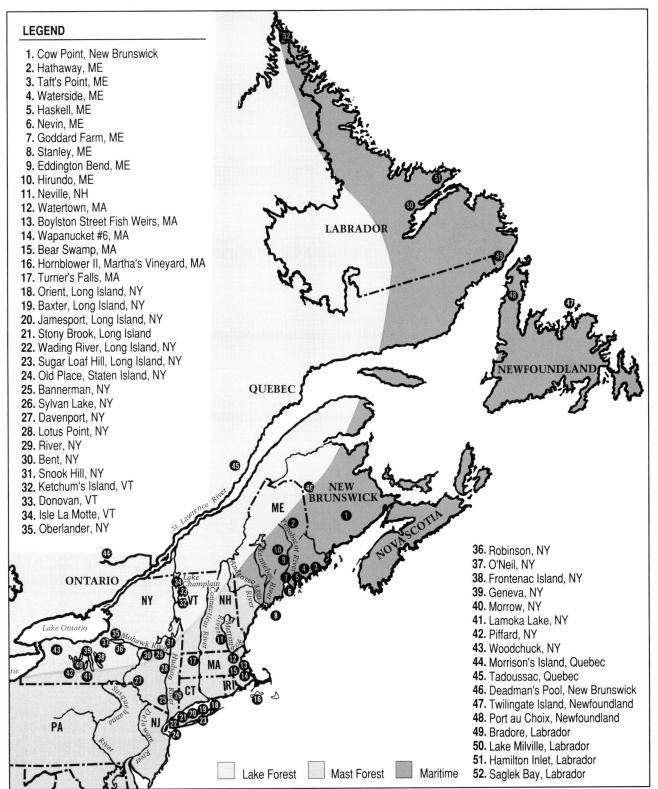

**LEGEND**

1. Cow Point, New Brunswick
2. Hathaway, ME
3. Taft's Point, ME
4. Waterside, ME
5. Haskell, ME
6. Nevin, ME
7. Goddard Farm, ME
8. Stanley, ME
9. Eddington Bend, ME
10. Hirundo, ME
11. Neville, NH
12. Watertown, MA
13. Boylston Street Fish Weirs, MA
14. Wapanucket #6, MA
15. Bear Swamp, MA
16. Hornblower II, Martha's Vineyard, MA
17. Turner's Falls, MA
18. Orient, Long Island, NY
19. Baxter, Long Island, NY
20. Jamesport, Long Island, NY
21. Stony Brook, Long Island
22. Wading River, Long Island, NY
23. Sugar Loaf Hill, Long Island, NY
24. Old Place, Staten Island, NY
25. Bannerman, NY
26. Sylvan Lake, NY
27. Davenport, NY
28. Lotus Point, NY
29. River, NY
30. Bent, NY
31. Snook Hill, NY
32. Ketchum's Island, VT
33. Donovan, VT
34. Isle La Motte, VT
35. Oberlander, NY

36. Robinson, NY
37. O'Neil, NY
38. Frontenac Island, NY
39. Geneva, NY
40. Morrow, NY
41. Lamoka Lake, NY
42. Piffard, NY
43. Woodchuck, NY
44. Morrison's Island, Quebec
45. Tadoussac, Quebec
46. Deadman's Pool, New Brunswick
47. Twilingate Island, Newfoundland
48. Port au Choix, Newfoundland
49. Bradore, Labrador
50. Lake Milville, Labrador
51. Hamilton Inlet, Labrador
52. Saglek Bay, Labrador

Lake Forest    Mast Forest    Maritime

Figure 25: A small map of the Northeast and surrounding regions can show only some of the many Late Archaic sites archaeologists have found. For example, archaeologists have discovered over 200 Late Archaic sites in and around the city of Boston alone, and they suspect that, as the result of the growth of the city, another 200 or more have been buried or destroyed. Archaeologists in the Northeast are able to find Late Archaic sites just about everywhere. The locations shown on this map are only approximate. (After Dincauze, 1979; Ritchie, 1980; Snow, 1980; Tuck, 1978a.)

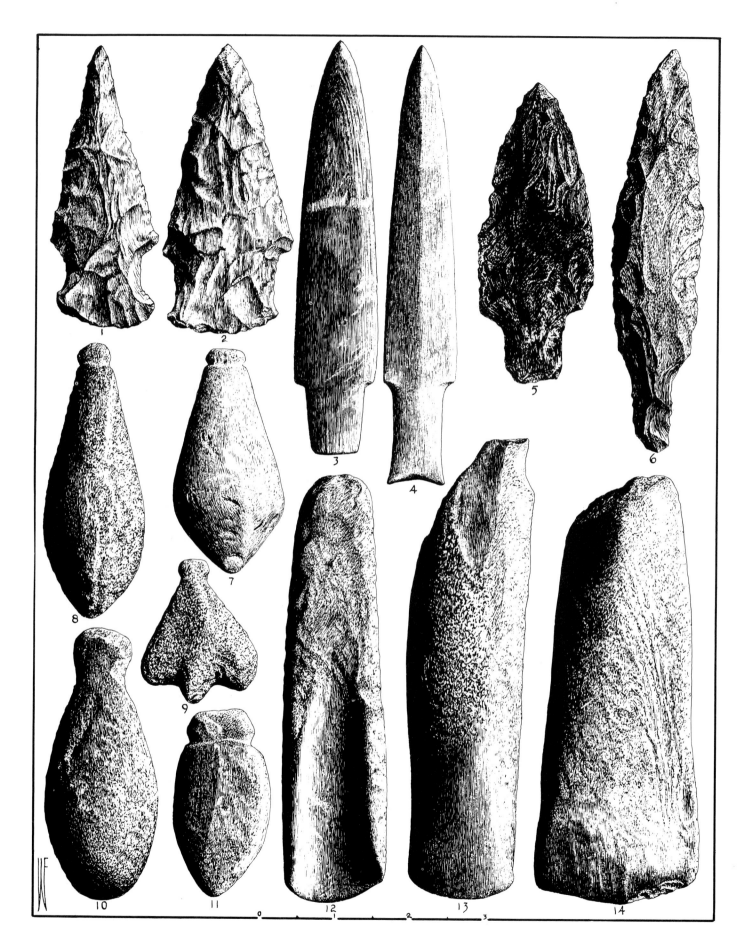

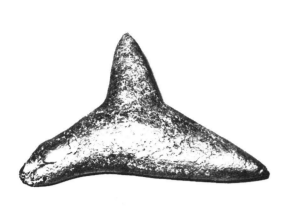

Figure 26: (a) (Opposite) Maritime Archaic sites in Maine contain many tools made by grinding down blocks of slate, as well as from stone. The gouge and adzes probably were used to carve wood, perhaps into canoes, other tools, or parts of houses. (Numbers 1, 2 daggers; 3, 4 slate points; 5, 6 points; 7, 8, 10, 11 plummets; 9, bird effigy plummet; 12, gouge [14 cm. (5.5 in.) long]; 13, 14 adzes. )
(b) (Above) Excavations at the Maritime Archaic site of Port Au Choix, Newfoundland, uncovered tools and carved objects made of stone. This site gives us our earliest glimpse of religion in the ancient Northeast, although archaeologists are not sure what the evidence tells us. Some possibilities are that the people made carvings of birds or of animals, including this whale effigy, as food for the dead, or as totems for special spirits. The people placed beads made of animal teeth and claws with the dead. They left red ocher (a powder made from a kind of iron ore) and beautiful stones in the graves. All of this may have had special meanings about which we can barely guess. (Drawings for Figure 26(a) by William Fowler for the Bulletin of the Massachusetts Archaeological Society, reproduced with permission. Photograph for Figure 26(b) courtesy of the New York State Museum.)

sites long before our laws and attitudes changed to recognize and respect the Native American dead.

Archaeologists in Maine also have excavated at sites where the people actually lived, adding to what we know of their way of life. The Maritime Archaic people of Maine had abundant food year-round. Archaeologists have found the remains of large camps, both at the shore and in the interior forests, where large groups of people gathered together year after year for many years. As far as we can tell, the ways of life in Newfoundland and in Maine were very much alike.

These people probably traveled into the interior mostly by dugout canoe. For this reason, archaeologists think the most important campsites in the interior were located along rivers large enough for such canoes. The people also camped at other, smaller sites across the interior lands, in places reachable only by

foot. The people also paddled out on the seas to hunt sea mammals and go after ocean fish—even swordfish! They must have been very skilled in using their canoes.

The Maritime Archaic way of life began sometime during the Middle Archaic, before 4,000 B.C. (6,000 years ago), and ended shortly after 1,500 B.C. We really do not know why it ended. Coastal sites after 1,500 B.C. contain more shellfish remains, and fewer bones of ocean fish. Also, there are fewer of the heavy woodworking tools than before. From these pieces of evidence, we can guess that fishing and hunting out on the seas, and carving large dugout canoes for ocean travel, became much less important. In addition, sites in the interior forests after 1,500 B.C. contain tools more typical of those of the Lake Forest Archaic way of life.

People did not leave the far northern lands after 1,500 B.C. They only changed the way they lived. Archaeologists believe the Late Archaic people in the northeastern parts of our region may have been the ancestors of the Algonquian speaking peoples of later times, many of whose descendants still live there today.

## The Lake Forest Archaic

People first developed the Lake Forest Archaic way of life further to the west of our region, around the Great Lakes. Sometime after 4,000 B.C., other people began to adopt this way of life all across southeastern Canada, northern New York, and Vermont. Archaeological finds in the interior of New Hampshire and Maine show us that some Lake Forest Archaic people also traveled still further east.

The people of the Lake Forest Archaic were masters of using their waters both for travel and for bringing in food. At some campsites, they caught migrating fish and sometimes also sea mammals that came up from the Gulf of St. Lawrence. Most of the people, however, obtained their food by fishing on the interior freshwater streams, lakes, and ponds. In the forests, they hunted quail, turkey, deer, woodland caribou, beaver, elk, bear, moose, and otter; around the numerous wetlands they hunted ducks, geese, and loons. In addition, they gathered many nuts and fruits in the forests.

During most times of the year, in contrast to the people of the Maritime Archaic, the people of the Lake Forest Archaic had lived in smaller camps scattered throughout their forests. Some lakes and rivers, however, were especially good places to catch fish during the warmer times of the year. Here, the people of the

## Life in Maritime Archaic Cycle

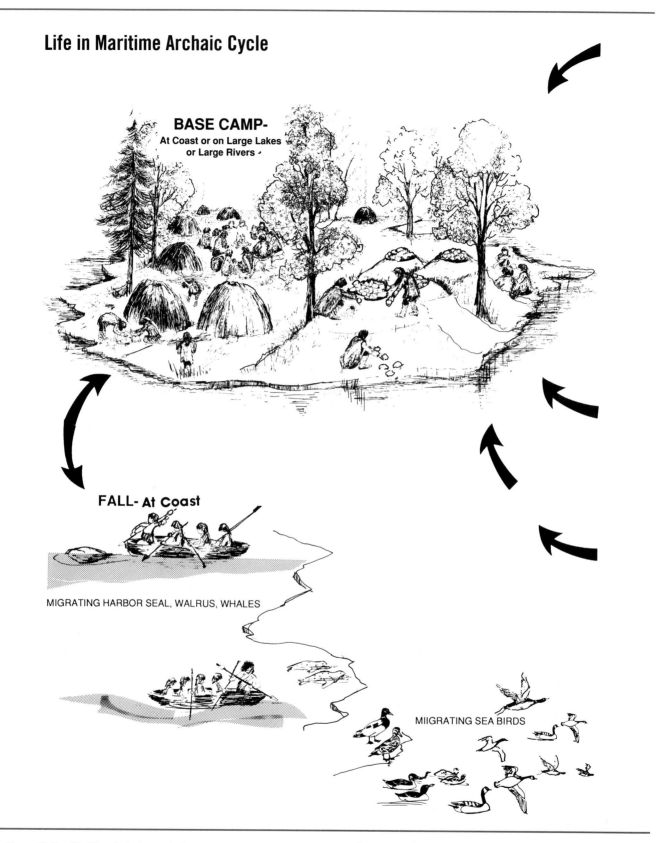

**BASE CAMP-**
At Coast or on Large Lakes
or Large Rivers

**FALL- At Coast**

MIGRATING HARBOR SEAL, WALRUS, WHALES

MIIGRATING SEA BIRDS

Figure 27: The Maritime Archaic people followed a regular cycle of gathering, hunting, and fishing in different places through each year. The sites we have found show that they often returned to the same places year after year, both on the coast and in the interior forests, following the cycle of the seasons.

SWORDFISH,

HARBOR SEALS

**SUMMER- At Coast**

**SPRING-**
At Coast or on Large Lakes
or Rivers

MIGRATING SALMON

MIGRATING HARBOR SEAL, WALRUS, WHALES

MIGRATING SEA BIRDS

**WINTER- Interior Forests**

## Life in the Lake Forest Late Archaic

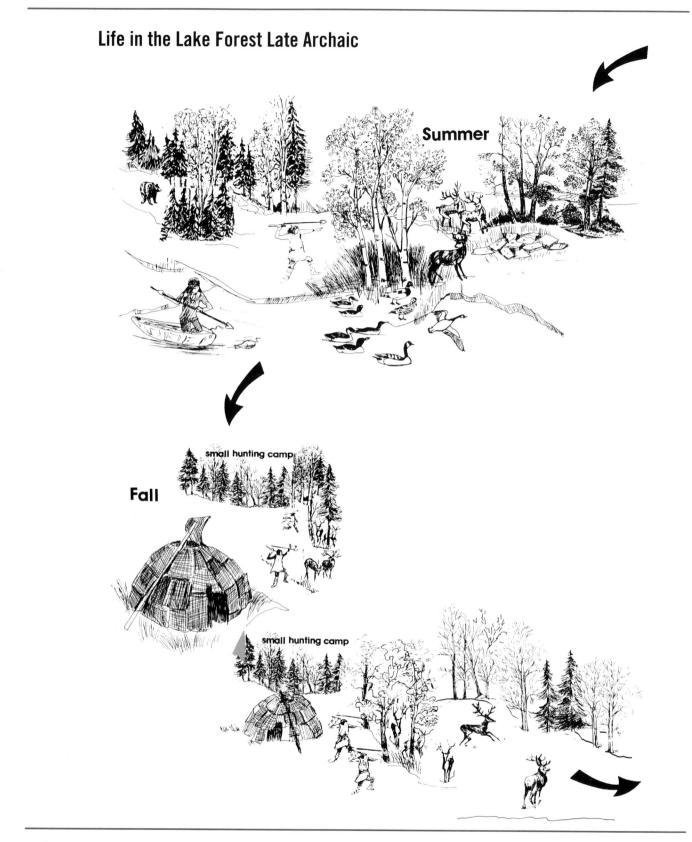

Figure 28: The Lake Forest Archaic people followed a regular cycle of collecting plant materials, hunting, and fishing in different places through each year, as did the people of the Maritime Archaic. They often returned to the same places year after year, especially places with the best fishing.

**Spring**

**Winter**

Figure 29: The Lake Forest people used much the same types of tools as did their neighbors to the east and south: tools for hunting and fishing, butchering meat and working hides, carving bone and wood, and for preparing plant materials for food or other uses. They used distinctively shaped spear points, which had large notches in their sides; these were probably for hunting deer and other land game, rather than for fishing. Their fishing tools show us that they brought in fish both by spearing and by using the hook and line. As with the people of the Maritime Archaic, they made some of their stone tools out of slate. (Clockwise, from the left: gouge [18 cm. (7 in.) long], for carving wood; hammerstone; plummet or fishing weight; ulu or curved knife; bannerstone or atlatl weight; two projectile points.) (Photograph courtesy of the New York State Museum.)

Lake Forest Archaic often came together, and here they also kept their main cemeteries.

Archaeologists found one especially large campsite on Frontenac Island in Cayuga Lake, New York. Although they did not find traces of any houses, the archaeologists found that people indeed had returned here year after year during the warmer months. A cemetery at Frontenac Island seems to contain several distinct groups of burials, which may be from separate families who kept their own burial plots, generation after generation.

The Lake Forest people sometimes cremated their dead, and sometimes they sprinkled red ocher over the grave. They buried their dead with small tools and ornaments, including objects made out of copper and out of the shell of a particular kind of conch. The copper came from the shores of Lake Superior; the shell from the shores of the southeastern United States. The finds of copper and conch shell in the Northeast thus show that the Lake Forest people traded with their neighbors to the west and to the south. By trading with people in other regions, the people of our region must have learned about how others lived. What they learned would eventually change their lives in several important ways.

Figure 30: The Lake Forest people of Frontenac Island in New York State made beads, combs, and other ornaments out of bone, stone, copper, and seashell. They also made flutes out of long bird bones and rattles out of turtle shells. (From left to right: bear tooth pendant, beaver incisor, bone needle, bone pendant, bone needle, decorative point [13 cm. (5 in.) long].) (Photograph courtesy of the New York State Museum.)

## The Late Archaic in the Southern Interior Forests

The people living in the more southern parts of our region lived in slightly different ways from one another, depending on whether they lived near the ocean or stayed in the interior forests.

Archaeologists have studied many Late Archaic sites in the southern interior forests. The best known of these is the Lamoka Lake site in south-central New York (see the map, Figure 25). Lamoka Lake probably is the site of the main village for a group of people who thrived in this part of our region around 2,500 B.C. (4,500 years ago). A "village" is a place where several families built their houses near each other and perhaps acted together as a community. People could live in a village year-round or only for some seasons of the year; the houses of a village might be built near each other along short trails, or they might all be built around an open plaza.

The Lamoka people and their neighbors to the south and east harvested the rich bounty of nuts provided by their forest's oaks (and probably also chestnuts and hickories), and they were skilled fishers and hunters. They gathered and then stored acorns in large pits, and they roasted them over large, open beds of coals. White-tail deer, turkey, passenger pigeon, and seemingly every kind of freshwater fish imaginable gave them most of their meat. The people fished using nets, as well as with spears and hooks; they hunted using spears and possibly hunting dogs.

Many people lived in small groups and spread out at small campsites for at least part of the year. They camped alongside streams, lakes, and wetlands while they hunted, fished, and collected plants. Not every-one traveled all the time, however. People often remained together at larger sites during seasons when nearby food was abundant. Some people even stayed year-round at these larger sites or villages, such as at Lamoka Lake.

Archaeologists have found numerous carved bone beads and pendants at the Lamoka Lake site, which show us that the people liked to ornament themselves or their clothing. They also made bone flutes for music, and they carved many small objects that they may have used for gambling or in other games. Unlike their Lake Forest neighbors, though, the families at Lamoka Lake did not trade much with people to the south or west.

Figure 31: Archaeologists have put together a picture of daily life at Lamoka Lake in New York, site of one of the largest Late Archaic villages known anywhere in the Northeast. They have found the remains of many houses at the site; these remains show us that the houses were rectangular, measuring roughly 4 by 5 meters (12 by 16 feet). At times, as many as 25 families may have lived together at this site—perhaps 150 to 200 men, women, and children—and their dogs! (Photograph of diorama on display at the New York State Museum, Albany, courtesy of the Museum.)

Few people used the Lamoka Lake site after around 2,000 B.C., and the local people began to follow a way of life more like that of their northern neighbors. Perhaps, too, this change came because people moved in from the north and brought their habits with them, or a cooler climate may have forced the Lamoka Lake people to move southward, to another area where they could continue their preferred way of life.

## The Late Archaic Along the Southern Coasts

Unlike the people of Lamoka Lake, the people living along the lower Hudson River valley, in southern New England, and on Long Island, continued their dis-tinctive way of life for many more centuries. Their coastal valleys, estuaries, seashore, and the ocean provided a special mixture of foods and other materials. The Late Archaic people here left many sites, and they also seem to have reused some of these sites over and over, for many years at a time.

As with their Middle Archaic ancestors, the Late Archaic people of the southern coasts fished in estuaries and gathered shellfish in the coastal bays. The rate of rise of the ocean level had slowed down greatly by this time. This change allowed tidal flats to develop, and shellfish that prefer to live in tidal flats, such as clams and soft shell crabs, flourished. In addition, the people fished in the ocean and caught seals, although not nearly as often as did their Maritime Archaic neighbors to the north.

Figure 32: The Late Archaic people of the southern forests, such as the people at Lamoka Lake, used many different kinds of tools. Like their neighbors to the north, they had tools for preparing plants for many uses, as well as tools for hunting and fishing, butchering meat and working hides, and carving wood and bone. Unlike the people of the north, however, they seem to have fished often with nets as well as with spears and the hook and line. Their stone spear points also had a distinctive, narrow shape unlike that of their northern neighbors. (Clockwise from the top: birdstone or atlatl weight, antler flake, projectile point, scraper, beveled adze [11 cm. (4.25 in.) long]. Center, left to right: biface and netsinker.) (Photograph courtesy of the New York State Museum.)

Figure 33 (Opposite): In 1913 and 1940, construction workers uncovered as many as 65,000 ancient stakes of wood, parts of a Late Archaic fishing weir—or perhaps several weirs—buried under filled-in land in Boston. This "Boylston Street Fish Weir" once covered several acres in the Charles River estuary. By studying this site, archaeologists have formed a picture of what it was like when the Late Archaic people gathered here to use their weirs. Part (a) in this illustration shows what a weir may have looked like at low tide; part (b) shows how some of the larger fish may have been speared once they were caught in the weir. Imagine the clamor as the fish were brought to shore to be cleaned and cooked; dogs barking for the scraps; everyone working together. Unfortunately, archaeologists have not found any sign of the big campsite that also must have been nearby. Perhaps it, too, lies buried under Boston. (Photograph for Figure 33a is of a diorama at The New England, Boston, Massachusetts, courtesy of The New England. Photograph for Figure 33b is of a painting on display at the Royal Ontario Museum, Toronto, provided by and reproduced with the permission of the Museum.)

a

b

The Late Archaic people of the southern coasts used fish weirs among their many new tools. A fish weir is a trap made out of hundreds or even thousands of stakes of wood, placed like a fence across part of an estuary. Each rising tide would bring schools of feeding fish up into the estuary; as the tide receded, its currents would pull some of these fish into the weir. A large weir could catch many fish at once.

The Late Archaic people of the southern forest and coasts developed another important new tool, a stone bowl carved out of soapstone—a soft stone that can be

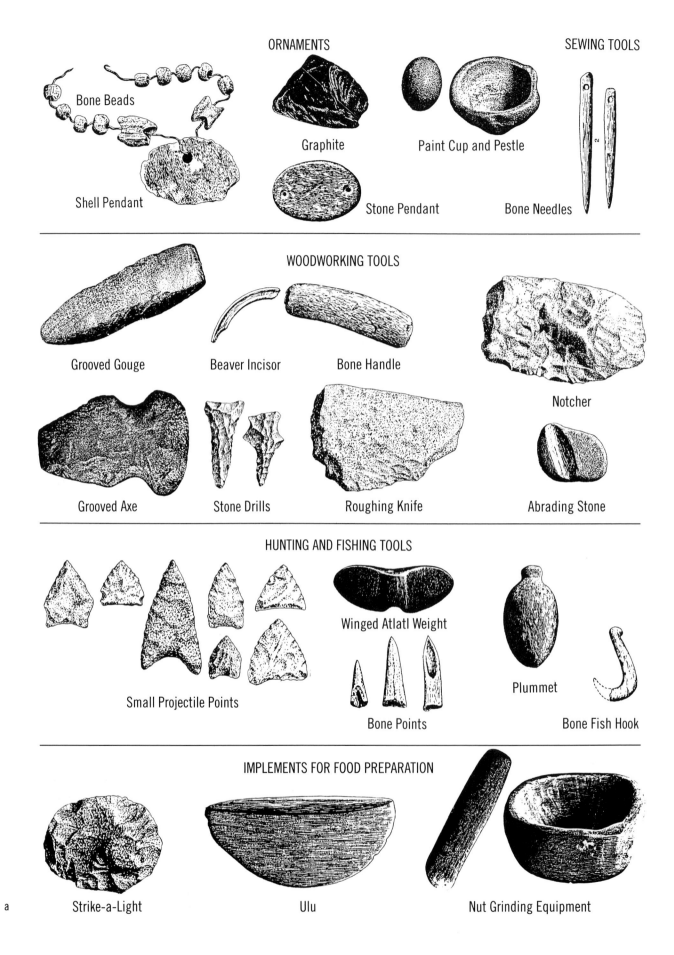

ORNAMENTS

SEWING TOOLS

Bone Beads

Shell Pendant

Graphite

Stone Pendant

Paint Cup and Pestle

Bone Needles

WOODWORKING TOOLS

Grooved Gouge

Beaver Incisor

Bone Handle

Notcher

Grooved Axe

Stone Drills

Roughing Knife

Abrading Stone

HUNTING AND FISHING TOOLS

Small Projectile Points

Winged Atlatl Weight

Bone Points

Plummet

Bone Fish Hook

IMPLEMENTS FOR FOOD PREPARATION

Strike-a-Light

Ulu

Nut Grinding Equipment

a

b

c

Figure 34: The tools left by the Late Archaic people of Long Island and southern New England tell us a lot about their way of life. Many stone and bone tools were made for fishing, others for hunting, and still others for grinding nuts and berries. These people fished using hooks, nets, and bone or stone-tipped spears; they hunted using spears tipped with distinctive, narrow stone points. They made fire by rubbing a hard stone like flint or quartz, called a strike-a-light, against a stone of iron pyrite. Archaeologists have found strike-a-lights and pyrite at sites of the Lake Forest Archaic people as well. The drawings in Figure 34 (a) (Opposite) show several kinds of tools from southern New England; Figures 34(b)-34(d) show some of the Late Archaic tools found in the area of Concord, Massachusetts, including (b) a grooved axe (13.5 cm. [5.25 in.] long) used for woodworking, (c) a plummet (7.4 cm. [3 in.] long) used for fishing and a winged spearthrower (9.8 cm. [3.75 in.] long) used for hunting, and (d) a mortar (8.7 cm. [3.5 in.] across) and grinding stone used for food preparation. (Drawings for Figure 34a are by William Fowler for the Bulletin of the Massachusetts Archaeological Society, reproduced with permission. The photographs for Figures 34b-34d are from Blancke and Robinson, 1985; the artifacts in the photographs are from the collections of the Concord Museum, Concord, Massachusetts, except for the spearthrower in Figure 34c, which is from the collection of Charles W. Dee; all are reproduced with the permission of the Concord Museum, and Figure 34c is reproduced also with the permission of Mr. Dee.)

d

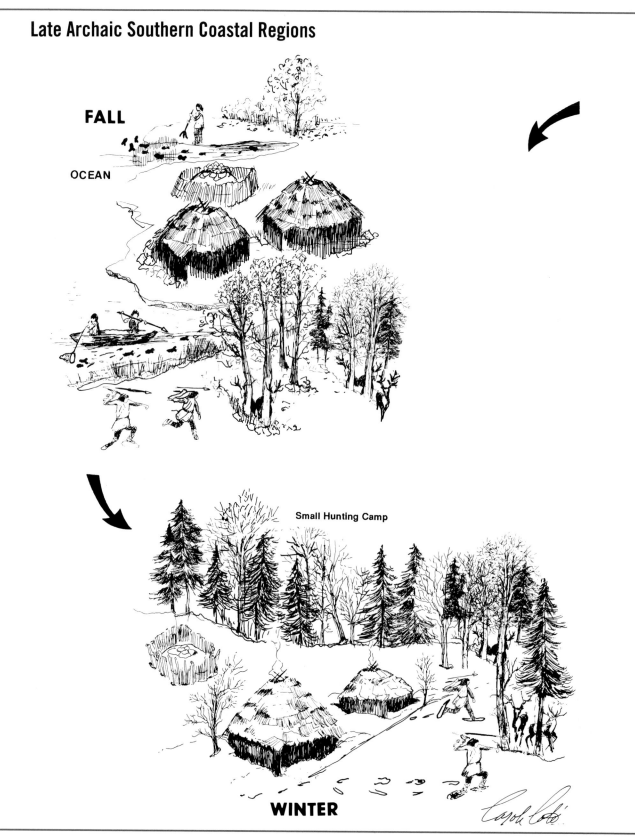

**FALL**

OCEAN

**Small Hunting Camp**

**WINTER**

Figure 35: The Late Archaic people of the southern coasts lived for at least part of the year in large campsites or villages. They also traveled along the coast and throughout the forests to gather nuts, berries, and other plant foods in season; to hunt and fish; and to collect shellfish.

SUMMER

MARSHLAND

SPRING

MAIN VILLAGE

OCEAN

Figure 36: Soapstone bowls were new but the people probably had long known how to make bowls out of birchbark and wood. Late Archaic people may have made their soapstone bowls in the same shapes as their other bowls, which have not survived. The stone bowls were flat bottomed and had handles. They ranged from 14 to 46 centimeters (5 to 18 inches) in width. The bowl in this photograph measures 13 cm. (5 in.) wide and 6 cm. (2.25 in.) high. (Photograph courtesy of the New York State Museum.)

found in only a few places in the Northeast. Archaeologists do not know how these bowls were used; at best, perhaps we can find clues by studying the Eskimos, who still used the bowls in recent times. The Eskimos used their bowls as lamps for burning oil, but they did not use them for cooking. They preferred to cook by "stone boiling"—they heated hand-sized rocks in a fire and then placed them in a skin or bark container filled with foods to cook. The Late Archaic people of the southern forests also cooked by stone boiling.

Archaeologists can tell that people cooked by stone boiling by examining the many broken hand-sized rocks left behind; cooking rocks often can break after being heated or after being dropped into a container of food. Late Archaic sites in the southern forests of the Northeast sometimes contain large numbers of these kinds of broken rocks.

The stone bowls made in the Northeast, though, are larger than the ones used by the Eskimos, and some even have burned bottoms, so perhaps they were sometimes used for cooking. But if so, what did they cook? We do not know yet. We do know that these people mostly left their soapstone bowls at sites along the warmer, southern valleys and along the coast. Perhaps they were used to cook foods found only in these warmer parts of the region.

Like the people at Lamoka Lake, the Late Archaic people of the southern coasts often gathered in large campsites or villages. These villages were near estuaries or large lakes or streams. A village site called Wapanucket 6 on Lake Assawompsett in southeastern Massachusetts contained the remains of seven Late Archaic houses. Unlike the houses at Lamoka Lake, these houses were round, and they had doorways with side walls to keep the winds from blowing inside. The houses had more than three times as much room inside as did the houses at Lamoka Lake. Each house had enough room for several close-knit families. One of the houses had over twice as much room as any of the others. Archaeologists question whether it was a place where everyone in the village could gather, or perhaps the home of the village leader. It may be that the Late Archaic people of the southern coasts stayed together at their main campsites only seasonally, rather than year-round.

These Late Archaic people of the southern coasts cremated their dead. We can tell very little of their health or diet from the few burned bones that remain. The people put many stone and bone tools in their graves, however, and these give us a glimpse of their way of life. Like the northern Lake Forest Archaic people, Late Archaic people along the southern coast buried their dead with materials from many distant regions—stone from the south and west, copper from far to the west, and seashells from far to the south.

Figure 37: Archaeologists think that as many as 100 people lived at Wapanucket 6 in southeastern Massachusetts. A cemetery of cremation burials was found nearby, perhaps the remains of some of the former residents of the village. Archaeologists and artists have built a model depicting what they believe was the daily life in this village. (Drawing by William Fowler of a diorama on display at the former Bronson Museum, Attleboro, Massachusetts, reproduced with permission. Diorama will be reconstructed at the Robbins Museum, Middleboro, Massachusetts.)

Figure 38: The people living along the southern coasts during the later centuries of the Late Archaic period made and traded a distinctive kind of stone spear point, called either the Atlantic or Susquehanna point. (Top row: Susquehanna points. Bottom row: Orient Fishtail points [bottom, far right: 8 cm.(3.25 in.) long].) (Photograph courtesy of the New York State Museum.)

Indeed, like their Laurentian neighbors to the north and west, the people of the southern forests and coasts did not simply keep to themselves. The soapstone used for their bowls came from only a few spots, so the people must have traded with each other for the stone, or for the bowls themselves. The Late Archaic people of the southern forests and coasts also built close ties with other groups who lived further to their south. We know of these ties because people living across a 500-mile-long region—from southern New England and south-central New York southward—

began to make broad spear points in a similar way. They also traded some of these stone points with each other, up and down the coast and along the major river valleys that reach to the coast. Perhaps these people swapped the stone points as gifts, to make friends with each other, or they may have actually moved from one region to another. If so, all we have left from these friendships are a few of their gifts.

This, then, was the Late Archaic period in the Northeast. It was a time of change in the ways of life of the people who came to live in our region. Although the changes were great, even greater changes took place in other parts of the continent and also very far away, in Europe. Those changes eventually affected how people lived, even in the Northeast.

# 5

# The Early and Middle Woodland Periods

While the Archaic people of the Northeast followed lives of gathering, fishing, and hunting, great changes were underway. These changes began far to the west and south, but they eventually touched even our region. The period of these changes in the Northeast is called the Woodland period. It began around 1,000 B.C. and ended with the arrival of Europeans in the A.D. 1500s.

Archaeologists divide the Woodland period in the Northeast into three parts: "Early Woodland," between 1,000 and 0 B.C.; "Middle Woodland," between 0 B.C. and A.D. 1000; and "Late Woodland," from A.D. 1000 to 1500. Peoples' lives changed in many ways during the Early and Middle Woodland periods, but they changed even more during Late Woodland times. We will look first at the Early and Middle Woodland times together.

## Distant Changes

During the Archaic period, people in what are now Mexico and Peru began growing some of the wild plants they liked to eat. Perhaps at first by accident, but later by choice, these people changed how their plants grew, and they selected the sizes of the seeds and fruit they wanted to produce. This was the beginning of farming in the Americas. Over many centuries, the ancient Mexicans and Peruvians slowly switched from gathering and hunting to growing practically all of their food.

Some of the first American crops were squash, pumpkins, gourds, beans, and a tall grass with tasty seeds, called teosinte. Year after year, people saved the seeds from their best teosinte plants and used these to grow the next year's crop. By doing this, the ancient farmers developed a new plant we would all recognize, corn! Maize, our name for this earliest corn, became the most important crop of ancient Central and South America (see Figure 40).

The ways of farming slowly spread across the Americas. After many centuries, Archaic people in eastern North America also started farming. The very first farmers in eastern North America lived during the Late Archaic in the broad valleys of the Ohio, Illinois, Mississippi, Tennessee, and Missouri rivers. These first farmers of the eastern forests did not grow maize or beans, though. They grew squash, gourds, and several plants that originally grew wild in their own valleys, including a plant still grown throughout the world today, the sunflower. It was not until much later, in the Woodland period, that the people of eastern North America began to grow maize and beans.

Archaic people in the eastern forests also discovered how to make pottery. As with farming, this new technique spread widely. The soapstone previously used for making vessels came from only a few places, but they could find clay for making pottery almost everywhere. Perhaps for this reason, people began to do more of their cooking with pottery, although some groups took to using pottery much more quickly than did others. Also, a few people continued to use soapstone, but only for a few special tools and only in places where the soapstone was easily found nearby.

The people of the eastern forests who took up pottery and farming began to stay in villages year-round and not travel so much to find food. Their populations

# Some Early and Middle Woodland Sites

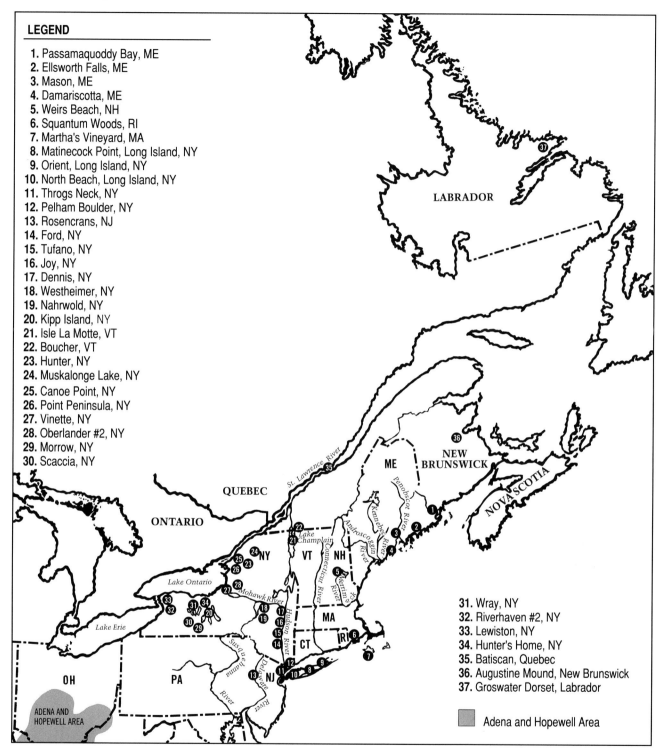

LEGEND

1. Passamaquoddy Bay, ME
2. Ellsworth Falls, ME
3. Mason, ME
4. Damariscotta, ME
5. Weirs Beach, NH
6. Squantum Woods, RI
7. Martha's Vineyard, MA
8. Matinecock Point, Long Island, NY
9. Orient, Long Island, NY
10. North Beach, Long Island, NY
11. Throgs Neck, NY
12. Pelham Boulder, NY
13. Rosencrans, NJ
14. Ford, NY
15. Tufano, NY
16. Joy, NY
17. Dennis, NY
18. Westheimer, NY
19. Nahrwold, NY
20. Kipp Island, NY
21. Isle La Motte, VT
22. Boucher, VT
23. Hunter, NY
24. Muskalonge Lake, NY
25. Canoe Point, NY
26. Point Peninsula, NY
27. Vinette, NY
28. Oberlander #2, NY
29. Morrow, NY
30. Scaccia, NY

31. Wray, NY
32. Riverhaven #2, NY
33. Lewiston, NY
34. Hunter's Home, NY
35. Batiscan, Quebec
36. Augustine Mound, New Brunswick
37. Groswater Dorset, Labrador

Adena and Hopewell Area

Figure 39: This map shows the approximate locations where archaeologists have found important Early and Middle Woodland sites in the Northeast. It also shows the areas to the west where people known to us as the Adena and Hopewell lived during these same times. Trade with the Adena and Hopewell people brought many new materials and perhaps new ideas into the Northeast during the Woodland period. (After Dincauze, 1979; Ritchie, 1980; Snow, 1980; Tuck, 1978a.)

grew; there were more and more villages, and some of these villages became quite large. Life in these settled villages was different. There were more people who had to get along with each other in each village, and more villages that had to get along with each other. It is not surprising that these peoples' lives changed in many ways. These changes began in the broad river valleys of the Midwest, but they took a while to spread into the Northeast. Slowly and eventually, though, life changed in the Northeast, too; it was these changes that made the Woodland period so different from the Archaic.

## Early and Middle Woodland Times in the Northeast

Life during the Early Woodland period in the Northeast at first differed little from life during the Late Archaic. Some people in our region began to use pottery around 1,000 B.C., but at first they did not use very much of it. People living all over the Northeast continued to bring in their food by gathering, fishing, and hunting long after they took up pottery. They did not begin farming for another 2,000 years.

Many sites where Early Woodland people lived contain no pottery at all, and archaeologists sometimes cannot tell if they belong to the Late Archaic or to the Early Woodland period, or even to both. As with their Late Archaic ancestors, Early Woodland people camped around the larger wetlands and lakes, along the larger river valleys, and on the coast at the mouths of rivers and streams. But soon, life began to change.

Archaeologists call the earliest pottery in the Northeast, Vinette I. These pots had very thick walls and lots of rough, crushed rock mixed into the clay. Potters everywhere like to mix their clay with such extra materials, called temper, to make their pots stronger. Vinette I pots stood only a foot tall or less, and they could hold about a gallon. Even empty, a Vinette I pot would have weighed several pounds—not something to carry around as easily as a basket.

With their thick walls and heavy temper, these pots would have broken easily if somebody put them over a very hot fire. They probably worked well only for simmering liquids over warm coals. One archaeologist working in Michigan has found evidence that the Early Woodland people there used their pots mostly to cook nuts down for their oil. In our region, archaeologists find Early Woodland pottery mostly in areas where nut-bearing trees could have grown. Perhaps the people of the Northeast and Michigan used their first

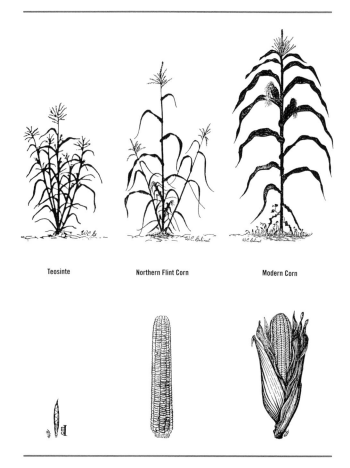

Teosinte        Northern Flint Corn        Modern Corn

Figure 40: The plants and ears of the earliest maize or teosinte were much smaller than those of modern corn. Flint Corn is a later kind of maize developed by the native people of eastern North America and grown by the Woodland peoples of the Northeast. Flint Corn had larger plants and ears than the earliest maize, but these still were smaller than those of modern corn. (Drawings by Walton C. Galinat, reproduced with his permission and that of American Society of Agronomy, Inc.; Crop Science Society of America, Inc.; and Soil Science Society of America, Inc.)

pottery in the same manner. Early Woodland people living in Maine found no use for pottery, perhaps because there were fewer nut-bearing trees in their region; people in Maine did not begin to make pottery until after 200 B.C.

The people of the Northeast at first did not decorate their pottery very much. Over the centuries, though, they found more and more ways to add decoration. They decorated the pottery by pressing variously shaped objects onto the clay before it dried. In this way, they could make a wide variety of designs. Then, once a pot was fired to make it hard, its design was set for good. Over time, people changed the way they made their pottery designs, and people in different areas often developed designs that were distinctly

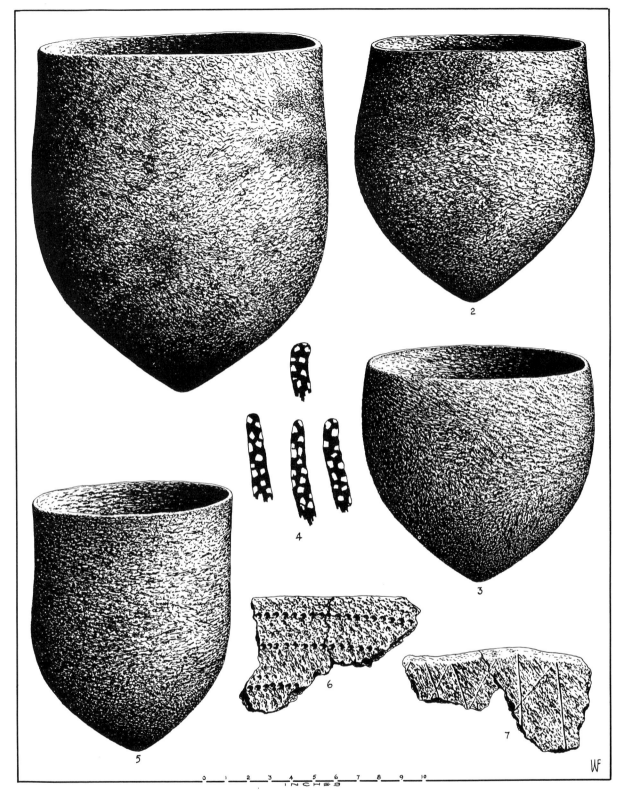

Figure 41: At first, people made pots shaped like baskets. After preparing the clay, a potter would mold it into the shape of a jar and then sometimes beat the still-damp jar with a small paddle wrapped in twine to give the surface a rough texture. When archaeologists uncover pieces of pottery, called sherds, they can see the impressions left by the twine on the potters' wrapped paddles. After a freshly made jar dried, the potter would place it in a hot fire to harden it. Here you can see drawings, based on sherds from several sites, showing what the oldest Northeastern pottery looked like. (Drawings by William Fowler for the Bulletin of the Massachusetts Archaeological Society, reproduced with permission.)

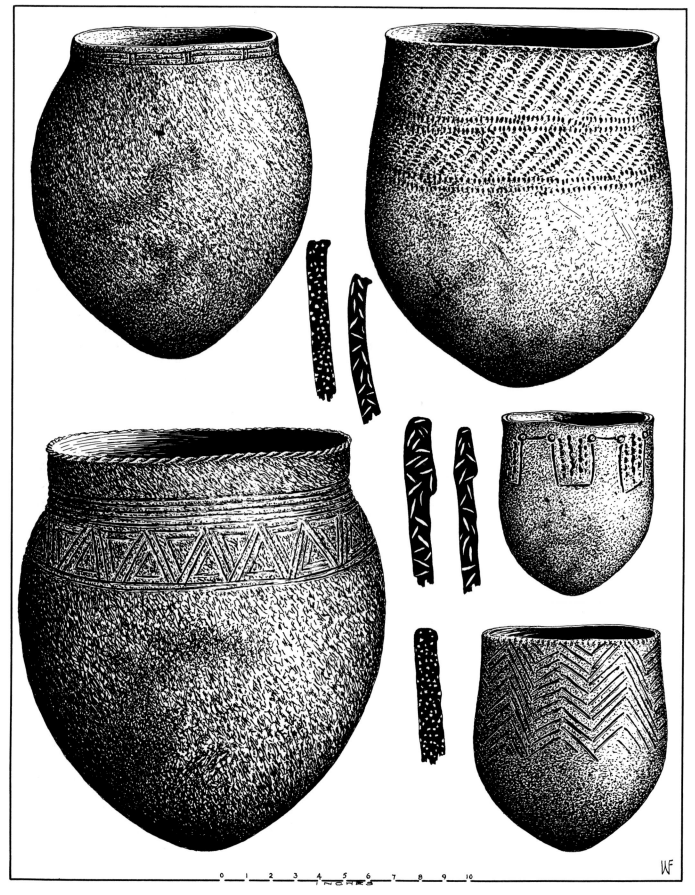

different from one another. Because of this, archaeologists often can tell roughly where and when a pot was made just by looking at its decoration.

Over the centuries, the people of the Northeast found ways to make larger, taller pots, with walls that were thinner than in Early Woodland times, but just as strong. These pots would have worked better for cooking over a hot fire. Archaeologists find pottery at almost all Middle Woodland sites in the Northeast, so we can guess that using pots had become a regular part of daily life.

Figure 42 (Opposite): (a) Here you can see drawings of Middle Woodland pottery from several sites in the Northeast. (Below): (b) By Middle Woodland times, people in the Northeast had learned to use the coil method to make their pots, and they developed new techniques for decorating. Instead of working the pot surface with a wrapped paddle, they smoothed out everything with either their fingers or a plain paddle. Then they often would add fine decorations in bands running around the outside made by pressing specially shaped objects into the drying clay. (Drawings for Figure 42b by William J. Howes and for Figure 42a by William Fowler for the Bulletin of the Massachusetts Archaeological Society, reproduced with permission.)

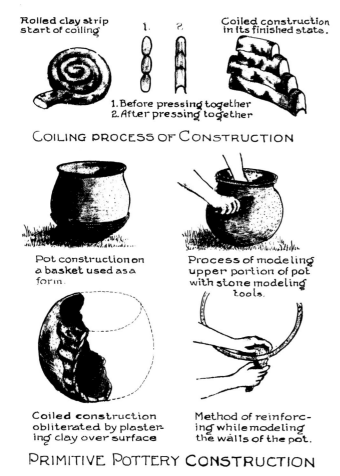

Rolled clay strip start of coiling

1. 2.

Coiled construction in its finished state.

1. Before pressing together
2. After pressing together

COILING PROCESS OF CONSTRUCTION

Pot construction on a basket used as a form.

Process of modeling upper portion of pot with stone modeling tools.

Coiled construction obliterated by plastering clay over surface

Method of reinforcing while modeling the walls of the pot.

PRIMITIVE POTTERY CONSTRUCTION

During Early and Middle Woodland times, the people also added new twists to the different ways of life developed by their Archaic ancestors. Especially in the western and southern parts of our region, people began to spend still more of their time each year—but perhaps not the entire year—in settled villages. Archaeologists once thought that families settled into villages because they had begun to farm the land. We now know that they did not begin farming in the Northeast until Late Woodland times. Instead, it looks as if people simply became more skillful at living on their land and so did not travel as far or as often from their villages as had their ancestors. They did still travel, of course, leaving traces of their visits at small campsites all across the land.

One of the new skills seems to have been storing food in large pits. People in the Northeast began using pits for storage during the Archaic period, but storage pits became much more common during the Early and Middle Woodland times, especially in western Vermont, New York, and southern New England. Archaeologists think that the people filled these pits with baskets of nuts, seeds, and dried berries during the late summer and fall of each year. With these stores of food to tide them over, people could get through the hard winter months more easily than before.

A more settled life brought other changes. Trade became a more important part of life. The Archaic people around Lake Champlain and in northern New York had traded with each other and with their neighbors both to the south and to the west as far away as the Great Lakes region. By the end of the Archaic, people from the coast of Maine to southern New York and New England were all trading with each other and with their neighbors to the south along the mid-Atlantic coast. The Woodland people of Vermont, New York, and southern New England not only continued these trading patterns, but they also reached out to others far to the west, in the Ohio River valley. By this time, the people of this distant valley had already started farming and living in larger, more permanent villages.

Early Woodland people in the Northeast traded with villagers living in southern Ohio, known to archaeologists as the Adena people. Later, their Middle Woodland descendants traded with the descendants of the Adena, whom archaeologists call the Hopewell people (see Figure 39). The Early Woodland people who lived in western and central New York, as far east as the Mohawk valley, had especially close ties with people in the Ohio valley. They took on many new

Figure 43: The Meadowood people of central New York State left behind many objects brought in from far away, or made in elaborate shapes out of local material. Ornaments of copper and seashell resemble those traded by their Late Archaic ancestors. Carved, polished stone objects shaped like birds, often called birdstones, may have been personal ornaments or fancy weights. Hunters may have placed such weights on their atlatl sticks, both for display and to help make their spears travel faster. The people also wore other objects on a cord around their necks, such as the gorget and pendant shown here. (Clockwise from upper left: copper ulu [16 cm. (6.25 in.) long], copper celt, gorget, pendant, whistle, two pipes.) (Photograph courtesy of the New York State Museum.)

ways from the west, including ways to make their tools and bury their dead. They also received many gifts from the people to the west, gifts made of copper, seashell, and many kinds of stone. We do not know what gifts they gave in return.

Archaeologists call these Early Woodland people of central New York, the Meadowood people. They kept so many tools and ornaments from their Ohio valley friends, that archaeologists once thought people from Ohio itself must have lived here. We now know that the Meadowood people were not visitors from the west. They were local descendants of the Late Archaic people who had lived in this same area.

Meadowood people lived in much the same way as their Late Archaic ancestors: they harvested nuts, seeds, and berries from the forest; hunted many birds and mammals; and fished in the lakes and streams. Unfortunately, archaeologists have as yet studied only one large Meadowood camp site, known as the Scaccia site. When they excavated part of this site, they found many deep storage pits. They also found the remains of a house, about the same size as the Archaic houses at Lamoka Lake.

Early Woodland people living further to the east, along the Vermont shore of Lake Champlain, also had close ties to the west. They traded with their Meadowood neighbors and with other people across the Great Lakes region but otherwise lived very much like their Late Archaic forebears.

The ways of life in Vermont and northern New York gradually changed, as did the ways of life of their trading partners to the west. By Middle Woodland times, the people living in the Finger Lakes region, the Mohawk and Hudson valleys, and the valley of Lake Champlain traded for new kinds of objects from the west. These objects included specially shaped pipes carved out of stone. The Middle Woodland people in this part of our region also adopted new, "western" ways to decorate their pottery and shape their spear points. Archaeologists call this changed way of life, Point Peninsula.

The Point Peninsula people lived in large, settled villages more often than did their Early Woodland ancestors. The sites of these villages often contain thick layers of trash with many pieces of fire-cracked rock and broken pottery. Some sites have a great many firepits and storage pits, and sometimes hundreds of postholes. There can be so many postholes from the houses built and rebuilt at the site, that archaeologists often cannot tell which postholes belonged to which houses. From the houses we can tell apart, we know that they were large. One had circular walls and measured over 6 meters (6.5 yards) across; another had a rectangular shape, over 6 meters long and nearly 4 meters wide. Perhaps these Middle Woodland people lived in larger households than did their Early Woodland forebears.

The Point Peninsula people were skilled at fishing with spears, nets, and the hook-and-line. They also hunted white-tail deer and collected enormous numbers of nuts, acorns, berries, and wild grapes. And they gathered seeds from a weedy plant known as 'lambsquarters' or 'Chenopodium.' Middle Woodland people living in Ohio and other parts of eastern North America raised crops of lambsquarters long before they learned to grow maize. We do not yet know if people in the Northeast also grew lambsquarters for food, or if they simply collected it wild. It still grows wild in the Northeast today.

Across southern New England and the New York coast, Early and Middle Woodland people followed

Figure 44: The tools of the Meadowood people consisted of stone spear points as well as bone and stone tools for hunting and butchering, for catching and cleaning fish, for making tools and clothing, and for preparing nuts and berries for eating. They probably used their pots (see Figures 41 and 42) to simmer stews. (Clockwise, starting from top left: two Vinette I sherds, knife [13 cm. (5 in.) long], drill, strike-a-light, two projectile points, scraper.) (Photograph courtesy of the New York State Museum.)

Figure 45 (Above): At many Early Woodland sites in the Northeast, such as the Boucher site along the Vermont shoreline of Lake Champlain, the people used cigar-shaped pipes carved out of stone. It seems that these people smoked tobacco or perhaps other kinds of leaves and bark. They had learned the pleasures, but not the dangers, of smoking. (Photograph by Louise Basa, reproduced with permission.)

Figure 46 (Below): Point Peninsula people who lived along the Hudson River became especially skilled at spearing sturgeon, a huge fish that once migrated up and down the river. These people made unusually large, heavy stone knives. Some archaeologists think these knives were made just for carving sturgeon. The knife on the right measures 6 cm. (2.5 in.) in length. (Photograph courtesy of the New York State Museum.)

ways of life similar to those of their Meadowood and Point Peninsula neighbors, but with some special differences. These people did not have such close ties with the distant villages in Ohio. They did trade with their closer neighbors, though, and also with people along the mid-Atlantic coast. This trading also brought in a few objects from the far west. Pipes from Ohio, for example, were traded all the way over to sites in eastern Massachusetts.

The people along the southern valleys and coasts adopted only a few western ways of making their tools. Their pottery in particular was unlike that made by their Meadowood and Point Peninsula neighbors. Perhaps because they lived near the coast, the people along the southern valleys and coasts used crushed seashells as temper in their pottery. They also sometimes wrapped pieces of their fishing nets around their pots before the pots dried, leaving impressions of the netting as decoration.

Life along the southern valleys and coasts was closely tied to the sea, much as in Late Archaic times. Many sites contain large shell heaps filled with shells of oysters, scallops, soft-shell clams, and quahogs. These shell heaps also have preserved the bones of many other food animals: land mammals, sea mam-

Figure 47: The Kipp Island site was a large Point Peninsula site near the north end of Cayuga Lake in central New York. Unfortunately, grave robbers and construction for the New York State Thruway destroyed most of the site before archaeologists could study it carefully. Tools found here and at neighboring sites include many different kinds made of stone and bone. These tools were used for hunting, fishing, butchering, preparing plant foods, and woodcarving, as well as for making basketry, nets, and clothing. The pottery, used for cooking, shows many different designs. (Outside, clockwise, starting in the upper left: antler chisel [19 cm. (7.5 in.) long], two ceramic sherds, fishing weight, pipe. Inside, top row: bone awl, pendant, harpoon, beaver incisor; bottom row: two projectile points.) (Photograph courtesy of the New York State Museum.)

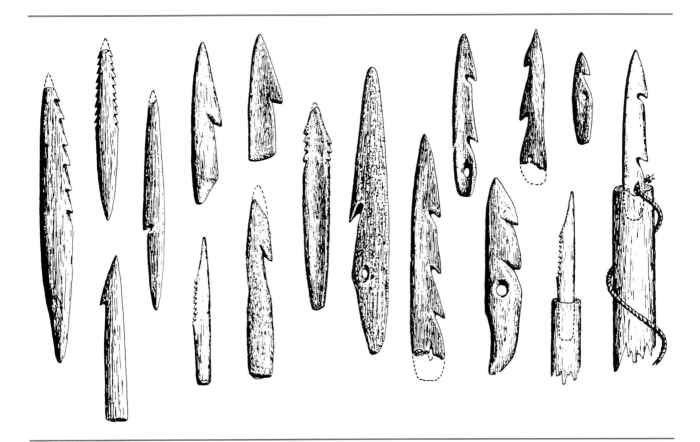

Figure 48: The tools made by the Middle Woodland residents of Maine, found at shell-heaps along the coast of Maine, include many made from bone and antler. Among these are harpoons in several shapes. This is evidence that fish and sea mammals of the coast continued to be important sources of food. (Drawings by William Fowler for the Bulletin of the Massachusetts Archaeological Society, reproduced with permission.)

mals, and birds, as well as fish from the lakes, rivers, estuaries, and ocean.

People sometimes settled year-round in villages near the coast. The sites of these villages have thick layers of trash with many pieces of fire-cracked rock and broken pottery, firepits and storage pits, and post-holes.

At one Middle Woodland site found on Martha's Vineyard, archaeologists uncovered traces of two large, circular houses, each of which measured about 5 meters (5 yards) across. Here, too, Middle Woodland people seem to have lived in large households. Archaeologists suspect that the people on Martha's Vineyard who used these houses visited the sites only seasonally throughout the year rather than living there year-round.

Life in the far northeastern parts of our region also changed during Early and Middle Woodland times, but

not in the same ways as in the rest of the Northeast. As already mentioned, the people living in Maine at first found no use for pottery. They did not begin to make pottery until around 200 B.C. The tools made by the Middle Woodland residents of the Maine coast also differ from those made by their neighbors to the south and west. These differences suggest to archaeologists that the people of Maine did not keep close ties with these neighbors. The Early and Middle Woodland people of Maine also used fewer woodworking tools than did their Archaic ancestors. From this, we can guess that they preferred to use lightweight birchbark canoes instead of dugout canoes.

By studying the kinds of animal bones and shells left in the trash at Woodland sites in Maine, archaeologists have found that some people either stayed at or visited sites near the coast throughout most of the year. These coastal residents may have used their harpoons to hunt sea mammals and large fish along the coast's numerous rocky reefs. They traveled into the interior forests only during the warmest months of the year.

Along the coast, the Middle Woodland people of Maine built houses by first digging a large, shallow pit with a flat bottom. They then built walls and a roof over the pit to create a "pit-house." These pit-houses

Figure 49: Birchbark canoes would have made it easier to move about in the interior forests. They would have been easy to handle on the swift and rocky streams, and easy to carry over the portages between the waterways. (Photograph courtesy of the University of New Hampshire Media Center, Durham, New Hampshire, reproduced with permission.)

were oval, about 4 meters (4 yards) long, each with a sunken hearth near the entrance and benches along the walls. Ancient people in colder lands often built pit-houses, because they gave better protection from the wind and kept out more of the cold. The people of coastal Maine built their pit-houses in sheltered spots, open to the sun for most of each day, with hills behind them to block the coldest winds.

Less is known about the Early and Middle Woodland peoples of the Maritimes because of the small number of sites. Many sites may have been eroded or inundated by the greater rise of the ocean near the Bay of Fundy. As archaeologists carry out further investigations, we may learn more about the Native Americans of the far northeast. Newfoundland seems to have been occupied by Eskimo groups, which arrived on the continent at a later date and were unrelated to the other Native Americans.

The Early and Middle Woodland periods thus were times of slow change across the Northeast. People in all parts of our region shaped ways to live together in larger, more settled communities. Especially in the western and southern parts of the region, they used

more kinds of plant foods, began using pottery for cooking, and used large pits to store foods for the winter. Although these people could not have known it, they had set the stage for a period of great change after A.D. 1000, the Late Woodland period.

# 6

# The Late Woodland Period

During Early and Middle Woodland times, the village dwellers in the great valleys of the Midwest began to grow much of their food. At first they grew mostly squash and gourds, sunflower, lambsquarters, and some other North American plants. Sometime during the Middle Woodland period, however, people to their south introduced them to maize.

After A.D. 600 or so, the Woodland people of the Midwest began to grow more and more maize, and their villages grew in size and numbers. They also saved the seeds of maize plants that grew especially well in their fields each year, using these seeds to plant the next year's crop. By doing this over and over, they developed a new kind of maize that we call Flint Corn. Flint Corn grew much better in the eastern Woodlands than did its tropical ancestors. Much of the corn we grow in our own fields and gardens today is Flint Corn, although modern scientists have improved it even more. (Figure 40 shows you what this Flint Corn looked like.) The development of Flint Corn made it possible for Woodland people to grow maize much further north than ever before, and by A.D. 1000 people living in the Northeast began to grow it.

It was not just maize that brought changes to the Northeast, though. Sometime between A.D. 500 and 1000, western neighbors taught the people of the Northeast how to use the bow and arrow. Until this time, the people of the Northeast had relied on the spear and atlatl as their main hunting weapons—and perhaps their weapons of war as well. The bow and arrow are a deadly combination used for hunting and fishing—and for warfare, too. By A.D. 1000, most people in the Northeast had taken to the new weapon.

Growing maize and hunting with the bow and arrow brought still other changes. The people learned how to grow beans in the same fields as their corn. To

grow these crops, they had to move their villages to places with good soils, and then move them again when the soil wore out. But how could they do this and still stay near good places for hunting and fishing? And what if someone else claimed the land with the best soils? Once they started raising crops, the people had to store them—and guard the stores from animals and perhaps even other people. Also, Flint Corn is a sweet, starchy food; tooth decay became a problem. In addition, perhaps simply because there was more food, the population began to grow. We will now look at what these changes meant for the people in different parts of our region.

## Northern and Central New York

Most of the well known Late Woodland sites in the Northeast lie in northern and central New York; similar sites also have been studied in southern Ontario, Canada. This area of the Northeast is the home region of several tribes, including the Iroquois of central New York, who played important parts in the early histories of Canada and the United States. Elsewhere in the Northeast, cities have covered over the remains of many Late Woodland sites. Perhaps someday we will know as much about the Late Woodland people of the rest of our region, as we know about the Late Woodland people of upstate New York.

Late Woodland people in the Susquehanna valley and in central New York began growing maize by A.D. 1000-1050; people across the rest of New York and in southern New England began growing maize soon thereafter. At first, the groups living in northern and central New York continued to live mainly by gathering, fishing, and hunting, but over the years between A.D. 1000 and 1400 they came to rely ever more on

# Some Late Woodland Sites

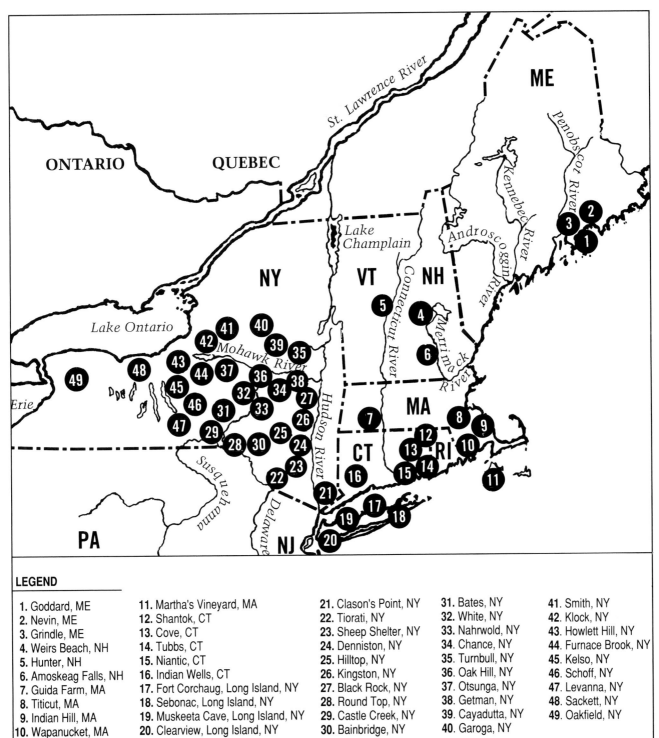

## LEGEND

| | | | | |
|---|---|---|---|---|
| 1. Goddard, ME | 11. Martha's Vineyard, MA | 21. Clason's Point, NY | 31. Bates, NY | 41. Smith, NY |
| 2. Nevin, ME | 12. Shantok, CT | 22. Tiorati, NY | 32. White, NY | 42. Klock, NY |
| 3. Grindle, ME | 13. Cove, CT | 23. Sheep Shelter, NY | 33. Nahrwold, NY | 43. Howlett Hill, NY |
| 4. Weirs Beach, NH | 14. Tubbs, CT | 24. Denniston, NY | 34. Chance, NY | 44. Furnace Brook, NY |
| 5. Hunter, NH | 15. Niantic, CT | 25. Hilltop, NY | 35. Turnbull, NY | 45. Kelso, NY |
| 6. Amoskeag Falls, NH | 16. Indian Wells, CT | 26. Kingston, NY | 36. Oak Hill, NY | 46. Schoff, NY |
| 7. Guida Farm, MA | 17. Fort Corchaug, Long Island, NY | 27. Black Rock, NY | 37. Otsunga, NY | 47. Levanna, NY |
| 8. Titicut, MA | 18. Sebonac, Long Island, NY | 28. Round Top, NY | 38. Getman, NY | 48. Sackett, NY |
| 9. Indian Hill, MA | 19. Muskeeta Cave, Long Island, NY | 29. Castle Creek, NY | 39. Cayadutta, NY | 49. Oakfield, NY |
| 10. Wapanucket, MA | 20. Clearview, Long Island, NY | 30. Bainbridge, NY | 40. Garoga, NY | |

Figure 50: This map shows the approximate locations where archaeologists have studied Late Woodland sites in the Northeast. If you compare this map to Figure 39, you will see that archaeologists know of many more sites from this period than from earlier Woodland times. (After Dincauze, 1979; Ritchie, 1980; Snow, 1980.)

Figure 51: People all over the Northeast began to make small, triangular points of stone for their arrow tips, using two basic shapes. When you see one of these points at a site, you can be almost certain it was made in Late Woodland times. The point on the bottom right measures 4 cm. (1.5 in.) in length. (Photograph courtesy of the New York State Museum.)

maize. We know this because tools for farming and for preparing and storing grain become common at sites from this time, and these sites also contain charred bits of corn. At some sites, archaeologists have even found the remains of gardens. Archaeologists call this Late Woodland way of life in upstate New York, between A.D. 1000 and 1400, the "Owasco" tradition.

The Owasco people also changed the way they made their cooking pots. At first they still made pots with tall, thick walls, and plenty of crushed rock for temper. Over time, though, these people found ways to make their pots with round, thin walls and finely crushed rock temper. These changes gave them pots that were better suited for boiling meals of grain over hot fires.

As the people of upstate New York came to rely more on maize, their populations grew, and they came to live together in larger and larger villages. Archaeologists have found village sites that covered as much as eight acres—about the size of eight football fields! Many hundreds of people lived in these large villages. Houses changed, too. In many villages, people began to build long houses with rooms for many families to live side by side. These longhouses were five to seven meters (5.5 to 7.5 yards) wide, and sometimes they reached over 40 meters (42 yards) from one end to

Figure 52: By the end of the Late Woodland period, the people of central New York made pots with thin walls, round bottoms, and high necks. They often decorated the necks with elaborate designs, including faces. The pot on the left is 16 cm. (6.25 in.) high. (Photograph courtesy of the New York State Museum.)

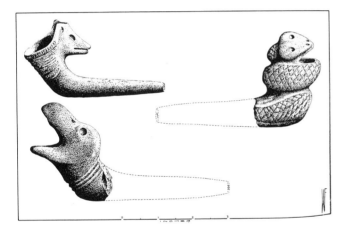

Figure 53: The Late Woodland people of central New York used a wide range of tools made of bone and stone. They wore many kinds of ornaments, and they made pipes out of clay, which they decorated with distinctive designs. (Drawings by William Fowler for the Bulletin of the Massachusetts Archaeological Society, reproduced with permission.)

Sometimes the people built mounds of dirt around their palisades, too. But why did they do this? Archaeologists have found the remains of villages that were burned to the ground, and the remains of people who died from arrow wounds. It seems that not everyone lived on good terms with each other. Perhaps they were fighting over the best land, or perhaps over the best places to fish and hunt, as their populations grew and grew.

Many villagers lived well with their neighbors, though. People in neighboring villages often decorated their pottery in similar ways, so they must have known each other well. Archaeologists have found groups of villages in some areas, where the people all made their pots in similar ways; used the same kinds of stone to make their tools; and lived along the same

Figure 54: By studying the remains of Late Woodland longhouses and Late Woodland tools, archaeologists have put together a picture of how the longhouses were built and what they looked like when they were finished. Working with museum artists at the Royal Ontario Museum in Toronto, Ontario, archaeologists have put together this scene of life in and around the longhouses of a Late Woodland village. (Photograph from the Royal Ontario Museum, Toronto, reproduced with permission.)

the other—room enough for seven or eight families at a time. Archaeologists think that the families of each longhouse were probably close relatives. Indeed, this was the way families in this part of our region lived when the first European visitors saw them.

Some villagers built palisades around their longhouses. These were high walls made of thick posts set closely in the ground, with only a few doorways.

Figure 55: Life in a palisaded village was probably noisy, smoky, busy, and crowded—after all, these were really small towns, with hundreds of people and many, many dogs. Imagine the sounds and smells of such a busy place! (Photograph courtesy of the Buffalo Museum of Science, reproduced with permission.)

Figure 56: By studying the remains of Late Woodland gardens, garden plants, and garden tools, archaeologists have put together a picture of how the people grew their crops. They planted the crops in groups of low mounds, growing maize, beans, and squash all together on each mound. This scene depicts a Late Woodland field in the Mohawk Valley of New York and is a diorama at the New York State Museum in Albany, New York. (Photograph courtesy of the New York State Museum.)

lakes, rivers, and valleys. Perhaps the people in each group of villages saw themselves as a distinct tribe, who looked out for each other and watched out for trouble from other tribes. Indeed, these groups of villages were probably the homes of peoples who later became members of the Iroquois Confederacy, and other groups who lived in the Northeast at the time the Europeans arrived.

## The Valleys of Lake Champlain and the Hudson River

Archaeologists have found numerous sites of Late Woodland villages all along the Hudson River valley and around Lake Champlain in both New York and Vermont. Sadly, though, many of these sites were destroyed by the spread of our cities and towns before archaeologists had the chance to study them. Because of this, we know very little about the Late Woodland people who lived in this part of our region. From the few sites that archaeologists have studied, we know that these Late Woodland people lived in much the same way as their Iroquois-region neighbors. They

probably belonged to different tribes, though; they used different designs on their pottery than did their neighbors to the west. When the Europeans arrived, they found that the people in this part of our region belonged to several tribes who sometimes fought with their Iroquois neighbors.

## Southern New England and Southern New York

Although we know less about them, too, the Late Woodland peoples living in southern New England and southern New York led lives similar to those of their western neighbors. They made their arrow points, pottery, and clay pipes in similar ways. Yet the people living in neighboring valleys often used different kinds of stone for their arrow points, and they decorated their pots and pipes with different designs. The Late Woodland peoples of southern New York and New England lived in several tribes, and these tribes probably did not keep close ties with their neighbors along the upper Hudson and Lake Champlain valleys or the valleys of central and northern New York. The Late Woodland peoples of southern New York and New England were probably the ancestors of the Algonquian tribes met by the first European visitors to our region.

Figure 57: The people of southern New England and southern New York made pots similar to those of their western neighbors. The pots had high collars, sometimes made with regular peaks called "castellations." The potters also decorated their wares by pressing and dragging specially shaped tools over the drying clay to create many different designs. They began to use crushed shell more and more often instead of crushed rock to temper, or strengthen, their pottery clays. At first they crushed the shell only coarsely; with time, they crushed the shell ever more finely and sometimes added fine sand or finely crushed rock to the mixture. (Drawings by William Fowler for the Bulletin of the Massachusetts Archaeological Society, reproduced with permission.)

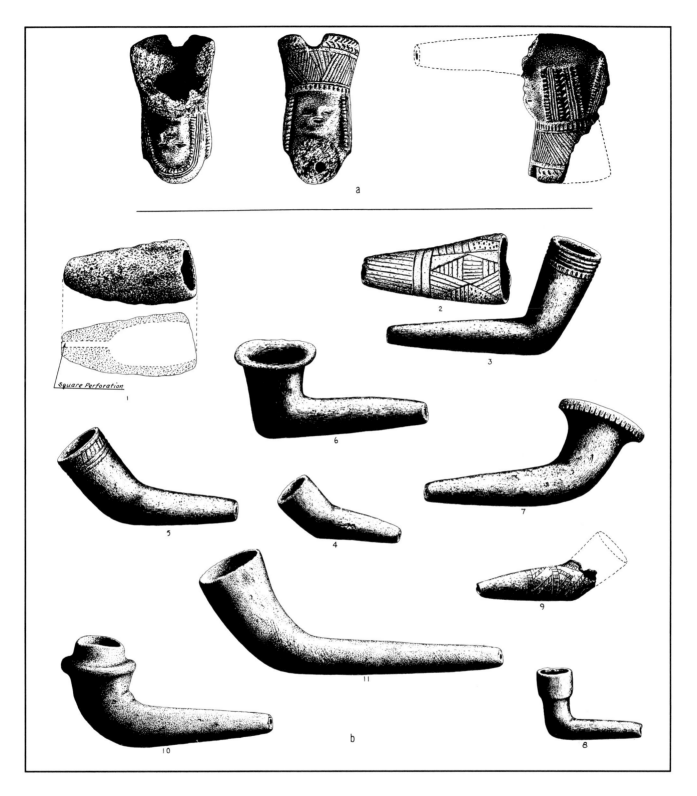

Figure 58: Late Woodland people in southern New England and southern New York also made highly distinctive clay pipes. As with their pottery, the people living in different parts of New England each made their own distinctive kinds of pipes and pipe decorations. Some people also made pipes carved from soapstone. Figure 58 (a) shows a ceramic Mohawk effigy pipe found in the Connecticut River valley. Figure 58 (b) shows other ceramic pipes found in southern New England. (Drawings by William Fowler for the Bulletin of the Massachusetts Archaeological Society, reproduced with permission.)

Figure 59: Late Woodland people in coastal southern New England sometimes lived in villages of about 100 people. Each family had its own circular wigwam of about 6 meters in diameter. Researchers have constructed this life-sized wigwam for an exhibit at Plimoth Plantation in Plymouth, Massachusetts. (Photograph from Plimoth Plantation, Inc., reproduced with permission.)

a

b

The Late Woodland people living in the southern parts of our region learned how to grow maize at just about the same time as their neighbors in central New York, but archaeologists are not sure just how quickly these people took to farming. We do know that they built their main villages near the coast and along the larger river valleys, often at an estuary or river rapids. Some people may have stayed at the main villages year-round, while others moved between the main villages and smaller, seasonal sites. Throughout the Late Woodland period, wherever the soils were good and there were enough warm days in the year for maize to grow, villages became larger and more numerous. This tells us that farming became more important, permitting larger and more permanent villages.

The pottery they made also tells us of changes in diet. As with the Late Woodland peoples of central New York, the people of southern New England and southern New York changed to making thinner, more rounded pots, but not as soon. From this, we can guess that farming did not become important as quickly in the southern valleys as it did in central New York.

The Late Woodland people who lived along the coasts of southern New England and on Long Island built their main villages around bays and estuaries close to shellfish beds. From their shell heaps, archaeologists have learned that these people ate deer and smaller animals; many kinds of birds, including turkey; seals and sometimes whales; many kinds of fish,

Figure 60: Among the tools of the Late Woodland people in southern New England were ground stone axes, celts, and gouges. These are all chopping tools, shaped for different tasks such as cutting, splitting, and smoothing large pieces of wood. They are just the kinds of tools you would expect to find among people who make dugout canoes. The villagers probably used these canoes for fishing, perhaps in both deep and shallow waters. Figure 60(a) shows a gouge (16 cm. [6.25 in.] long) and an axe from southern New York; Figure 60(b) shows a celt (13.6 cm. [5.25 in.] long) found in the area of Concord, Massachusetts. (Photograph for Figure 60a courtesy of the New York State Museum; photograph for Figure 60b from Blancke and Robinson, 1985, reproduced with the permission of the Concord Museum, Concord, Massachusetts.)

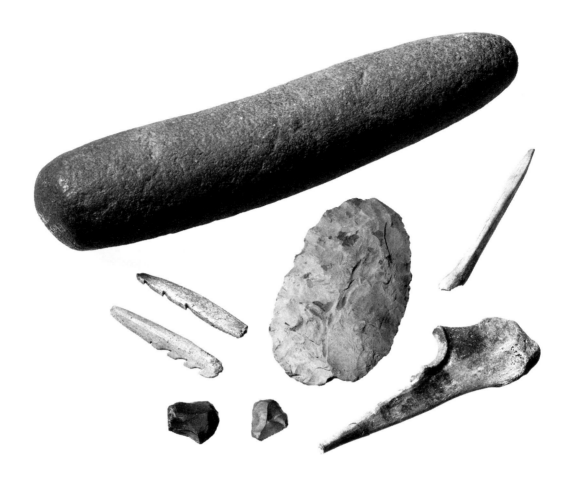

Figure 61: Common Late Woodland tools in southern New England included knives, scrapers, drills, adzes, arrowpoints, strike-a-lights, pestles, and net-sinkers; bone awls, barbed bone points, bone and shell fishhooks, and bone needles; antler flakers, beaver incisor chisels, and beads from fish vertebrae. (Clockwise, from the top: pestle [26 cm. (10.25 in.) long], two bone awls, two scrapers, two barbed points. Center: flint blade or knife.) (Photograph courtesy of the New York State Museum.)

including sturgeon; and several species of shellfish. They grew and ate some maize, but they still obtained most of their food by gathering, fishing, and hunting.

The Late Woodland villagers of the southern forests lived in both longhouses and round houses, which were called wigwams. Each wigwam measured about 6 meters (6.5 yards) across and it probably was home for one family. Several families probably lived in each longhouse. Archaeologists have found two different types of pits in their village sites. There are small, shallow pits that seem to have been used for baking shellfish; and there are larger, deeper pits that seem to

have been used for other types of cooking or storage.

One discovery on Cape Cod in 1979 deserves special mention. Construction accidentally uncovered a kind of burial called an ossuary, a large burial containing the bones of many individuals. The people here saved the bones of their dead and periodically collected them together. They then held a special funeral for all their ancestors. Such burials tell us that these Late Woodland peoples lived in strongly-knit groups with close ties to the same place over many generations. The scientists who rescued the site have returned the bones to Cape Cod for reburial by the remaining descendants of these Late Woodland people.

## Northern New England and the Canadian Maritimes

The Late Woodland people living in northern New England and the Maritime provinces did not live in the same way as their southern or western neighbors. The climate in Maine, New Hampshire, eastern Vermont, and the Canadian Maritimes was just too cold for growing maize. The inhabitants of these lands instead continued to live by gathering, fishing, and hunting, although they did not live exactly in the same ways as their Middle Woodland ancestors.

Middle Woodland people along the coast of Maine had lived mostly in villages of pit-houses near the coast, and they traveled back and forth between these villages and campsites in the interior forests. Something changed this way of life after A.D. 1000. The Late Woodland people of Maine lived more often at sites high up along estuaries, or at waterfalls or important points along the main rivers. They made only short trips to the coast and to the interior, apparently in lightweight birchbark canoes. They replaced their ancestors' pit-houses with small, round houses built out of poles and bark. Archaeologists are not sure why these changes happened.

These northern people did not change the way they made their pottery nearly as much as did their southern and western neighbors. They continued to make pots with thick walls and tall, barrel-like shapes much like those of Middle Woodland times. They did begin to crush shells for temper, but they never crushed them as finely as did their neighbors to the south or west. They also used less and less pottery as time passed. Perhaps their pots were just too heavy and fragile to carry around in birchbark canoes. Perhaps, too, they found that they did not have as much use for pottery as did their neighbors to the south and west.

Much less is known about these northern Late Woodland peoples than about those to the south and west. Because of extensive erosion and the rising seas around the Bay of Fundy, archaeologists have had the same difficulty finding sites as they had for earlier Woodland times.

The people of this area were probably the ancestors of the Maliseet-Passamaquoddy of Maine and western New Brunswick, and of the Micmac tribes of Nova Scotia, Prince Edward Island, and eastern New Brunswick. Newfoundland and Labrador became the home of Eskimo groups unrelated to these tribes.

## The End of an Era

By the middle of the 1500s, a few European explorers had "discovered" the Northeast. The native peoples they met were the Late Woodland peoples of the land. By the 1600s, the Europeans came to claim this land as their own. Their arrival brought about many drastic changes for the native peoples and their ways of life.

# 7

# European Contact

Our story ends with the colonization of the Northeast by Europeans, and with the many changes that followed. At the time the Europeans arrived, native peoples lived in small villages throughout the Northeast and especially along river valleys and the sea coast—some seasonally and some year-round. Archaeology can tell us some things about the ways of life of these villagers, and we can learn still more from the records kept by European explorers and early settlers.

## The Arrival of Europeans

Throughout the Late Woodland period, the people of Newfoundland and Labrador occasionally caught sight of some unusual visitors. These visitors appeared along the sea coast in strange boats with large mats stretched on tall poles to catch the wind. The visitors had light skins and faces covered with hair, which was sometimes black but sometimes light like their skins. It is difficult to imagine the thoughts of the northeastern peoples who first sighted these Europeans.

The first Europeans to visit the Northeast left few written records of their stay. Explorers from settlements in Iceland reached Greenland after A.D. 900 and from there reached Newfoundland around A.D. 1000. Settlers followed, founding a colony at L'Anse aux Meadows, from which they shipped wood and perhaps other goods back to Iceland. Hard times came during the late 1200s, however, and the visitors abandoned all of their American settlements by around A.D. 1300. They apparently had little contact with the natives. A Norse coin that was excavated at a Late Woodland site in Maine might be evidence that they explored other parts of the Northeast, although it could also have arrived there through trade.

These early explorations were soon forgotten, but Europeans again reached the Americas a few centuries later. By the 1400s, silks and spices and other goods from India and China were in great demand in western

Europe. Moslem Arabs controlled the long and difficult trade route that extended across Asia by land, and they would trade only with merchants from Venice and Genoa. Europeans from other cities dreamed of finding their own routes to India and China by sea. For years, the Portuguese had been searching for a sea route around the continent of Africa. Vasco da Gama, an explorer for Portugal, finally succeeded in discovering such a route around Africa to India in 1498.

While some Europeans thought the world to be flat, others believed that it was round and that they could reach India and China by sailing west across the Atlantic Ocean. Christopher Columbus was one who believed this. Sailing west in Spanish ships, Columbus instead reached the Americas in 1492. Convinced that he had reached the East Indies, he called the dark-skinned people who lived there "Indians." In fact, where he had expected to find the East Indies, China, or Japan, he instead found Cuba and Hispaniola, two islands in the Caribbean Sea.

News of Columbus' discovery brought great excitement to Europe. Jealous of Spain, other countries sent their own explorers to the Americas. Many of the first contacts between the native Americans and the Europeans did not go well for the natives. A ship from Portugal, for example, kidnapped 57 native people from Newfoundland and took them away as slaves.

While exploring the "new" lands, the Europeans also discovered the rich fishing grounds off the coasts of Labrador, Newfoundland, Nova Scotia, and New England. Beginning in the 1500s, Europeans came here more and more often to fish. At first the fishing crews did not need to make camps on the shore, as they could preserve the fish for the long voyage home by salting it right on board their ships. Eventually, though, some crews found it easier to preserve their fish by drying them at camps along the shore. Some of these crews camped along the eastern shores of our

# Northeastern Tribes Around 1600 AD

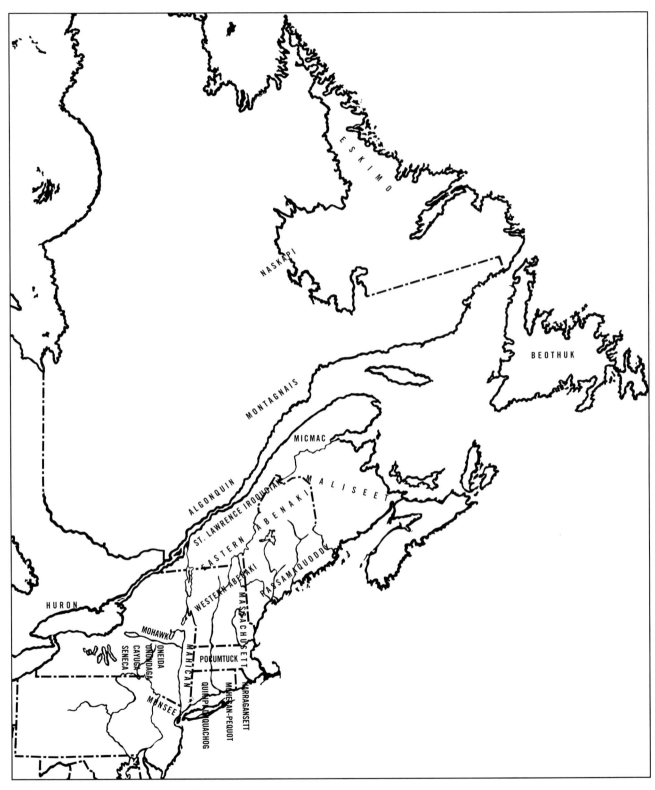

Figure 62: This map shows the approximate locations of the major groups of native peoples of the Northeast met by the Europeans. The names on the map were first recorded by the Europeans as they listened to the people and wrote down what they heard. (After Salwen, 1978; Snow, 1980; Tooker, 1978.)

region, and here the natives saw them more and more often.

The people at the European fishing camps and the native peoples around them got along well to start. The natives of the Northeast had long trapped beaver and other animals for their furs. When the Europeans saw the pelts, they admired them for their beauty and their warmth. Soon, wealthy Europeans began to demand hats and other fashionable items of clothing made with American furs. Travelers to the northern coasts of America began trading with the natives for the pelts, exchanging them for manufactured items such as iron tools, brass kettles, glass beads, and liquor.

Meanwhile, European explorers continued to investigate the "new" continent. Their encounters with the native peoples were often friendly, but sometimes they were violent. Verrazano, a Spaniard, explored the eastern coast of North America from North Carolina to Maine in 1524 and left us our first written account of such a voyage. He met "Indians" at several points along the way and found them mostly friendly and very curious. Verrazano wrote that the native peoples living around the mouth of what we now call the Hudson River greeted him and showed him good landing places. He also wrote of seeing many fires along the coast of what we call Connecticut, and of spending two friendly weeks with people at what we now call Narragansett Bay in Rhode Island. Verrazano did not receive such a friendly greeting in Maine.

During the same period as Verrazano's mostly pleasant meetings with natives, other explorers provoked different reactions. Crews from other Spanish ships, for example, began visiting the southeastern coasts of North America to kidnap native villagers and take them back to Spain as slaves. News of this violence spread up and down the coast and the natives became very suspicious of their visitors. Spaniards tried to establish a colony in North Carolina, in 1526, but the native peoples drove them out. During the 1500s, in fact, most attempts by Europeans to establish settlements on the coast south of our region also ended in failure. In some instances, natives massacred the settlers.

Europeans turned many of the native people to the south against them, but they were still able to fish and trade for furs along the coasts of the Northeast and the lands further north. For a while in the 1500s, French fishermen even lived with natives on some islands off the coast of Newfoundland. European whaling ships also visited the coast. During these same decades, the French began exploring and trading in eastern Canada, along the St. Lawrence River, and southward into the Hudson River valley.

By the 1600s, both the French and English had established successful settlements in the Northeast: the French in Quebec, New Brunswick, and Nova Scotia; the English in Maine. Still, none of these settlements lasted long, for several reasons. Many settlers were driven out by the harsh winters and, at one settlement, by a devastating fire. Elsewhere the settlers fell into conflict with each other and allowed their settlements to collapse. Still others ran out of money from their supporters back in Europe, and so they could no longer purchase shipments of needed supplies from Europe. Despite these failures of the settlements, though, the fur trade continued.

The English finally established a successful settlement under Captain John Smith on the shore of the Chesapeake Bay, Virginia, in 1607. These colonists managed to survive hostility and famine. From then on, the Europeans came in greater numbers and now often came to acquire land instead of furs and other goods.

The Dutch entered the scene in 1609. At first, their explorer, Henry Hudson, stole furs and other goods from native peoples on the Maine coast. Then, after sailing southward along the New England coast, he sailed up the river which was later named after him and traded with the Mohawk people. Dutch settlers arrived soon after word of Hudson's voyage reached home, and they began setting up trading posts. They established their first real colony at New Amsterdam, now New York City, in 1624. The Dutch settlers made every effort to be friendly, hoping to become important merchants in the fur trade themselves.

In what we call Massachusetts, some early English adventurers kidnapped several Nausets and Pawtuxets in 1614 and sold them into slavery in Spain. One of the Pawtuxet men kidnapped, named Squanto, later escaped to England. In 1619, he returned to New England on an English ship. But home had changed. All of his Pawtuxet tribe had died of European diseases.

Shortly after Squanto's return, a band of English people fleeing religious persecution landed on Cape Cod. These people, whom we call Pilgrims, upset the local Nausets by stealing their maize and opening their graves. The Nausets were hardly eager to have the English in their midst, both because of these un-

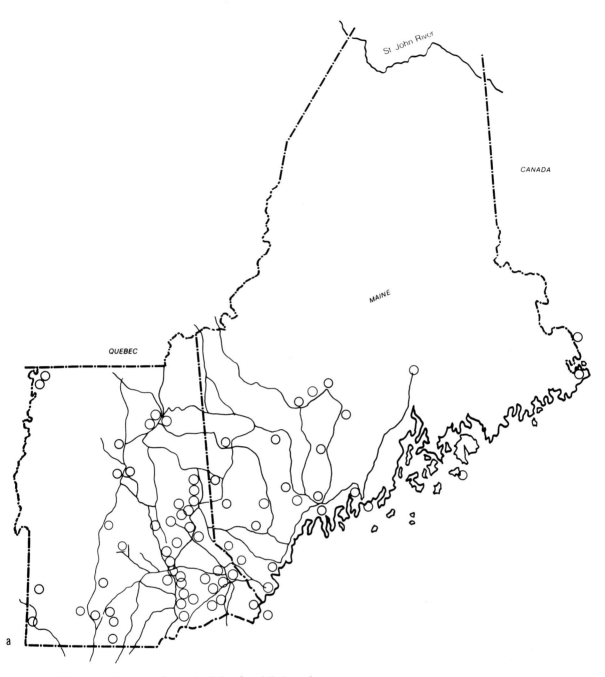

Figure 63: When the Europeans first arrived, they found that people traded with each other across the entire region over a network of well-worn routes. We know of at least the most important of these routes from records kept during the first two centuries after the Europeans arrived. Figures 63(a) (above) and 63(b) show the major routes in New England; Figure 63(c) shows the major routes in New York State. The circles on the maps indicate the locations of major villages or groups of villages. (Original maps for Figures 63a and 63b prepared for *Indian New England Before the Mayflower* by Howard S. Russell, reproduced with the permission of University Press of New England and his family. Figure 63c is based on Morgan, 1851; Thompson, 1966; Jennings, 1984; and Trigger, 1990.)

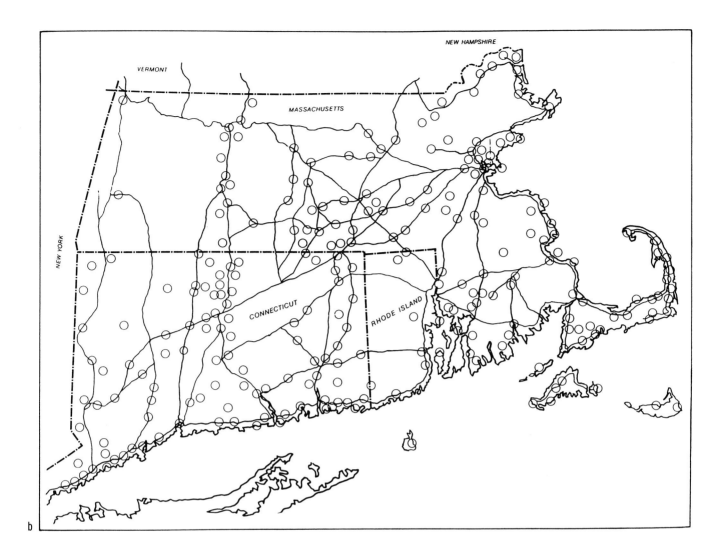

## Trade Routes and Villages in New York

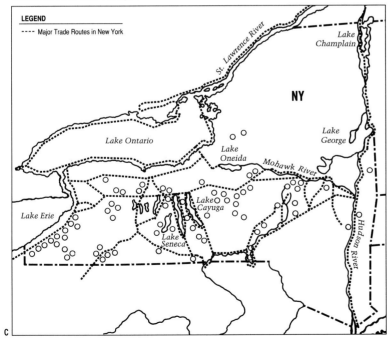

LEGEND
---- Major Trade Routes in New York

# Europeans in the Northeast in the Early 1600's

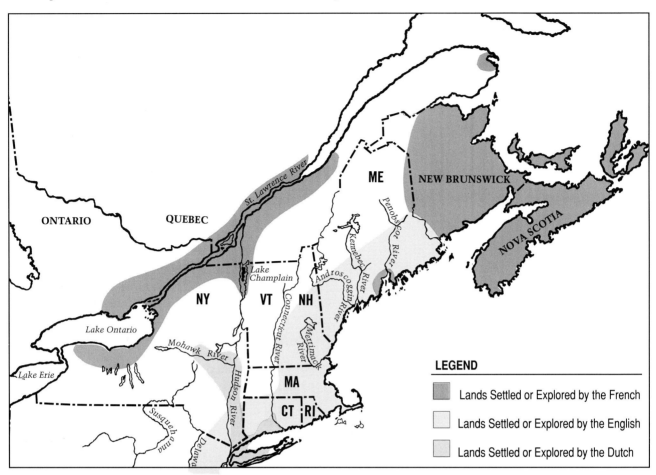

LEGEND

▉ Lands Settled or Explored by the French

☐ Lands Settled or Explored by the English

▨ Lands Settled or Explored by the Dutch

Figure 64: This map of eastern North America shows the approximate extent of European settlement and exploration in the early 1600s. (After Borraclough, 1979, and Shepherd, 1964.)

pleasant acts and because of the kidnaping five years earlier. The Pilgrims then sailed north into former Pawtuxet territory, where they established a settlement at Plymouth in December of 1620. Squanto, who had learned English during his captivity, introduced the Pilgrims to Massasoit, the leader or sachem of the nearby Massachusett people. Samoset, one of the Massachusett people, greeted the English by saying, "Welcome, Englishmen."

## The Peoples of the Northeast at the Time of Contact

Our account of the early years of contact between European colonists and the native people of the Northeast comes from the words of Europeans who visited or lived in the area. Samuel de Champlain, a French explorer of the early 1600s, for example, kept a detailed record of his travels along the coast, including descriptions of the land, the people, houses, and ways of life. Other original sources include: *History of Plimoth Plantation* by William Bradford, the colony's second governor; and *New England Prospect*, an account of life in the Massachusetts Bay Colony in the early 1630s written by William Wood, a resident of that colony.

William Wood, for example, described the villagers of northern Massachusetts and southern New Hampshire as "between five or six foot high, straight bodied, strongly composed, smooth-skinned, merry countenanced, of complexion something more swarthy than Spaniards, black haired, high foreheaded, black eyed, out-nosed, broad shouldered, brawny armed, long and slender handed, out breasted, small waisted, lank bellied, well thighed, flat kneed, handsome grown legs, and small feet." He found that his neighbors enjoyed good health and long lives, "most of them being fifty before a wrinkled brow or gray hair betray their age," despite their living in simple huts, wearing little clothing, working hard, and eating only simple meals.

He also described the hair styles of the men as "fantastical": "their boys being not permitted to wear their hair long till sixteen years of age, and then they must come to it by degrees, some being cut with a long foretop, a long lock on the crown, one on each side of his head, the rest of his hair being cut even with the scalp. The young men and soldiers wear their hair long on the one side, the other side being cut short....Other cuts they have as their fancy befools them, which would torture the wits of a curious barber to imitate." And yet, despite this fascination with the hair on the tops of their heads, they could not bear to have any hair showing on their faces, "where it no sooner grows but it is stubbed (pulled) up by the roots."

As people do throughout the world, the native peoples of the Northeast had their own medical practices using plants and plant extracts. Four hundred and fifty of their plant remedies and fifty drugs are the basis for some of our modern medicines. They knew how to heal fractures, using bark and resin as cement to set the bones. They knew how to cure frozen feet and reduce swelling. Fish oils and fats from other animals gave them protection against the sun, weather, and insects. Elderly, knowledgeable women usually prepared the medicines. The givers of cures used both the plant remedies and magic, along with chanting, drumming, and rhythmic dancing. Many people also used sweat baths in special wigwams as a pleasant way to cleanse, relax, and cure, especially during the winter.

The native people believed that everything natural deserved their respect and appreciation. They did not worship gods as idols, but as powers deserving respect. The sun, moon, winds, thunder, rain, and seas all had special powers. The people often buried their dead facing the southwest, the direction where they believed the soul went to feast with its ancestors. They usually buried the dead person with his or her most cherished possessions as well as with items to be used in the next life.

## Life in the Southern and Western Lands at the Time of Contact

The archaeological evidence shows that, when the Europeans first arrived, the natives of New York, western Vermont, and southern New England lived by farming, gathering wild plants, fishing, and hunting. The Europeans recorded that the people lived in villages joined together loosely into tribes. They called themselves by different tribal names, including Delaware, Mahican, Massachusett, Mohawk, Munsee, Narragansett, Nauset, and Pequot, to name but a few. Some of these tribes were bitter rivals with long histories of attacking each others' villages, sometimes over even the slightest of insults.

Each village was home to a group of related families. They usually built their settlements in places favorable for farming and fishing. Early European visitors remarked that the land was cleared for settlement all along the southern coast; on the off-shore islands; and inland along river valleys, ponds, and lakes. Shortly after 1600, Samuel de Champlain recorded his impressions of the native fields along the mouth of the

Figure 65: Villages consisted of several houses and were surrounded by gardens, as shown in this model at the Peabody Museum, Harvard University. The villagers built their houses out of long poles, which they bent over, tied together, and covered with bark and woven mats. Some houses were long and rectangular, others were small and circular. (Photograph from the Peabody Museum of Archaeology and Ethnology, Harvard University, reproduced with permission.)

Saco River of southern Maine: "We saw their Indian corn, which they raise in gardens. Planting three or four kernels in one place, they then heap up about it a quantity of earth....Then three feet distant they plant as much more, and thus in succession. With this corn they put in each hill three or four Brazilian beans (kidney beans), which are of different colors. When they grow up, they interlace with the corn, which reaches to the height of from five to six feet; and they keep the ground very free from weeds. We saw there many squashes, and pumpkins, and tobacco."

Figure 66: The residents kept fires going in one or more pits inside their houses. Over each pit they placed a forked stick for holding a cooking pot. They kept much of their equipment inside their houses, such as baskets, pots, gourd pitchers, and bark vessels; and they used mats, skins, or low platforms for sleeping. A hollowed-out tree trunk served as a mortar for grinding corn. (Photograph of diorama on display at the New York State Museum, Albany, courtesy of the Museum.)

The people in each village held their surrounding lands in common and worked some fields together to provide food for feasts and for guests. They also shared in using other parts of the land, including nut-tree groves, berry fields, deer-hunting areas, firewood groves, marshes for hunting and for collecting building materials, fishing stations on waterways, and shell-fishing areas along the coast. Entire villages sometimes would move when the people had exhausted the nearby soils and firewood supplies.

There were both differences and similarities in peoples' ways of life across the western and southern parts of our region. The tribes of central New York formed a confederacy, known as the Iroquois Confederacy, that acted as a single nation in their dealings with other tribes as well as with the Europeans. Each tribe consisted of several clans, each responsible for some particular activity within the community, such as trade

Table 1: Some of the many wild plants used by the native peoples of the Northeast.

*Plants Used for Food*

| *Spring* | *Summer* |
|---|---|
| fiddlehead ferns | strawberries |
| marsh marigold shoots | raspberries |
| cattail shoots | blackberries |
| milkweed shoots | blueberries |
| Jerusalem artichokes | grapes |
| | cranberries |
| *Fall* | black plums |
| chestnuts | cherries |
| hickory nuts | currants |
| walnuts | mulberries |
| acorns | wild leeks |
| | milkweed flowers |
| *Winter* | rose hips |
| roots | sassafras |
| stored nuts and seeds | sarsaparilla |

*Plants Used for Equipment*

hemp—for nets, lines, ropes, baskets
bayberries—for wax
witch hazel—for hunting bows
white pine—for dugout canoes
red cedar wood—for dishes
sweet flag—for roofing and caulking
red cedar bark—for twine and mats
sphagnum moss—for baby care
cattails—for thatching and weaving
hickory wood—for hunting bows
white oak wood—for dugout canoes, dishes

(Source: Russell, 1980.)

or warfare. Each clan had a male leader, who was selected by the women; the clan leaders served as a governing council for the villages and tribes. The women clan members could remove from office any leaders who behaved badly.

The native people of southern New England and southern New York also lived in villages and tribes. Each village had its own leader, either a man or a woman, as did the entire tribe, but the leaders did not have as much say over their people as did the Iroquois clan leaders. Councils of men and women also met to decide important matters, as in the Iroquois villages.

However, the villages and tribes were generally smaller than the tribes of central New York, and they never came together to form large and powerful confederacies like the Iroquois.

The people of the western and southern parts of our region did not keep many tools, because they moved so frequently within their tribal lands. They did have some heavy belongings, such as large ceramic jars and mortars. These they left in their main villages rather than carry them around as they moved to different campsites. They moved around by foot and by dugout and bark canoes; they did not ride on any animals or use any wheels.

People throughout the Northeast had been trading with each other for a long time before the Europeans came. With the arrival of the Europeans, this trade grew. Along the border between farming and non-farming areas, native peoples had long been exchanging furs for food produce, ceramic pots and pipes, maplewood bowls, and chestnuts. After the Europeans arrived, the native people used the same network to trade European-made goods as well.

With the growth of the fur trade, Europeans and native peoples both began to use shell beads, or wampum, as a kind of money. At one time, for example, three purple beads or six whites equaled one English penny. Some people continued to use wampum in this

Figure 67: In a few areas, the people built palisades around their villages for protection against raids from rival tribes and perhaps also from Europeans. (This drawing is part of a map of New Netherlands drawn in Amsterdam in the 1600s by Joannis Janssonius, reprinted with the permission of the Harvard Map Collection, Harvard University, Cambridge, Massachusetts.)

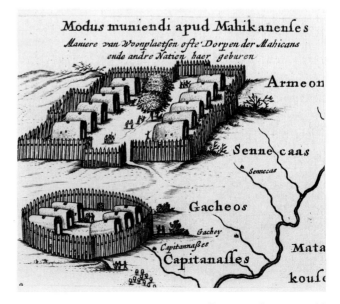

## Life in Central New York at the Time of Contact

**Spring**

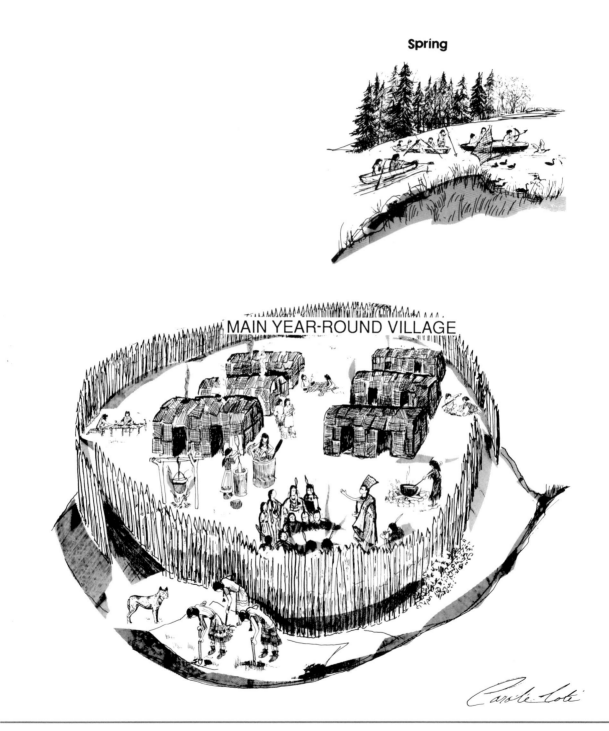

MAIN YEAR-ROUND VILLAGE

Figure 68: The people of the Iroquois Confederacy followed a way of life closely tied to the timing of the seasons for planting and harvesting their fields, for hunting and collecting nuts and berries in the forests, and for fishing along their waterways.

Summer

Fall

Winter

## Late Woodland Life in Southern New England

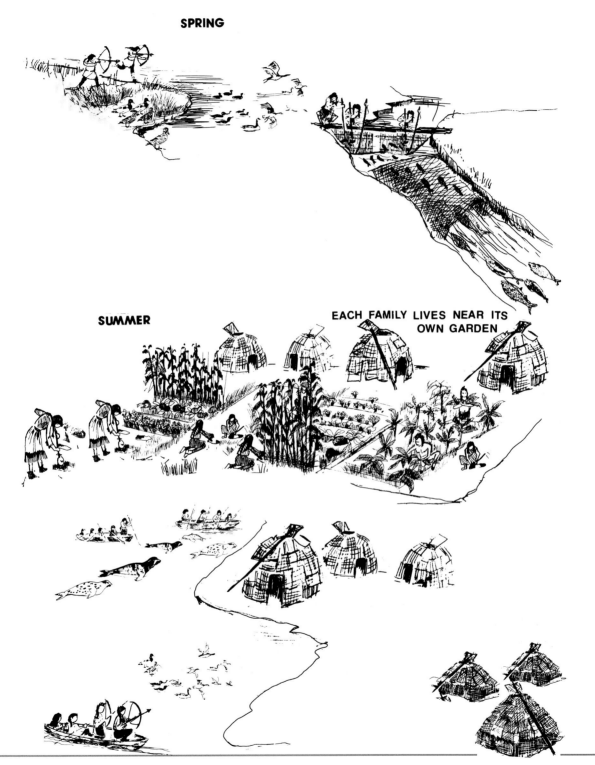

**SPRING**

**SUMMER**

**EACH FAMILY LIVES NEAR ITS OWN GARDEN**

Figure 69: The native farming people of southern New England and southern New York also followed a way of life closely tied to the seasons for planting, harvesting, gathering, fishing, and hunting. The ocean and estuaries provided a special bounty of foods and other useful materials. During the summer months, most people lived in small farmsteads and hamlets near the coast; during the colder months, they came together in their larger villages along the bays and around lakes near the coast.

MAIN VILLAGE

FALL

WINTER

People From
Other Villages

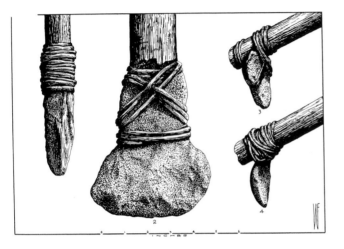

Figure 70: Growing crops required many different tools and the work of many people throughout much of each year. (Photograph of painting on display at the Royal Ontario Museum, Toronto, provided by and reproduced with the permission of the Museum; drawings of tools by William Fowler for the Bulletin of the Massachusetts Archaeological Society, reproduced with permission.)

way until the American Revolution in 1775. Wampum also was important in many ceremonies.

## Life in the Northern Lands at the Time of Contact

When the Europeans came, they found that the native peoples of the far northern and eastern parts of our region lived in different ways from their southern and western neighbors. We see these differences in the archaeological evidence, too. The far north was simply too cold for the native crops to grow well. Instead, people continued to live in small bands and to gather, fish, and hunt to get their foods. They kept their main villages alongside the larger streams, particularly at falls and estuaries. The city of Bangor, Maine, rests on

the site of one such village, which overlooked falls on the Penobscot River.

Without farming, the northern peoples did not over-work the land around their villages and so kept their villages in the same places for many years. Because they did not fight over who got the best land for growing crops, and because they lived far from the wars of their southern neighbors, the northern people did not live in palisaded villages. The northern people also kept small campsites away from their main villages, particularly in the forests for winter hunting and on the coast for summer fishing.

The northern people ate many wild nuts, seeds, and berries; and they used simple digging sticks to dig up groundnuts. They caught migratory alewife, shad, salmon, eel, and smelt that were on their way up-stream in the spring. They also fished for the salmon and eel as they migrated back to the ocean and harpooned sturgeon along their rivers. And they hunted deer, elk, moose, bear, and many smaller animals in the forests.

These northern peoples traveled their many streams in bark canoes, which were swift in the water and easy to carry over land. They also continued to make pottery in the old, short, conical shape; the pots probably were used for cooking nuts and stews, not corn. Once they started trading with Europeans, the northern people stopped making pottery and used only metal kettles.

Some native people of northern New England did try farming, mostly in southern Maine, but with little success. Only in the Presumpscot valley near Portland, Maine, did crops come in well; in good years, the people grew gourds, beans, peas, maize, flax, strawberries,

Figure 71: The main weapon for hunting and for warfare throughout the Northeast was the bow and arrow. (Photograph from the University of New Hampshire Media Center, Durham, New Hampshire, reproduced with permission.)

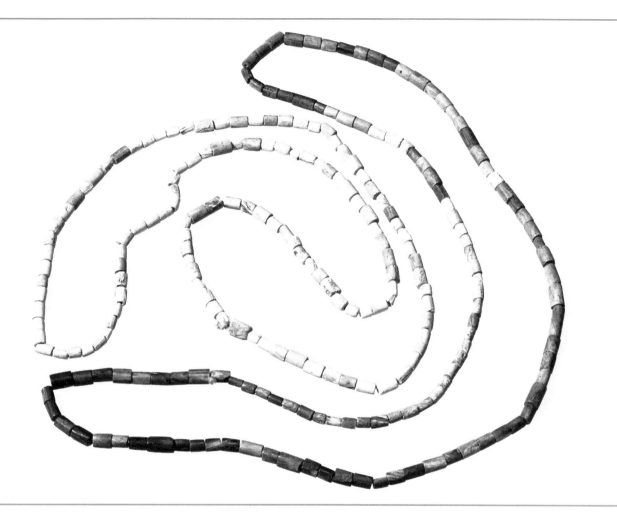

Figure 72: Ornaments in the Northeast included wampum belts and necklaces. To make wampum they sewed shell beads into large strings and belts. They also used shell beads to decorate their clothing and to weave into patterns in honor of special occasions. The most prized beads were purple, made from quahog shells from the southern coasts. Lighter beads were made from periwinkle or whelk shells. People made the beads by grinding pieces of shell into shape on stone slabs and drilling them with stone drills; later, they used iron drills obtained from the Europeans. The beads in these necklaces average about .5 cm. (.25 in.) in length. (Photograph courtesy of the New York State Museum.)

fruit trees, and nut trees. Even in this valley, though, the people could not count on a good harvest every year and relied mostly on gathering, fishing, and hunting. Once the Europeans began to trade for furs in their area, the people of the northern lands gave up trying to raise their own crops.

As did the people to their south and west, the native people of the northern lands recognized themselves as different tribes; they knew each other by names such as Maliseet and Passamaquoddy. Each tribe consisted of villages spread over a large territory.

Each village had a leader, whom the people chose for his ability to act fairly and wisely for the village. If people did not like the way a leader behaved, they could move to another village or try to force their old leader out. Sometimes one leader, called a sachem, would become the spokesman for all the villages in a region.

These northern New Englanders believed in shamanism. A shaman was a person with magical powers who could turn himself or herself into animal forms. Rare carvings on rocks along the Kennebec River show scenes of shamans changing themselves into other forms. We know little else of their religions. Pierre Biard, a Jesuit missionary, wrote in 1616 that, when someone died, the people tied the dead person's body up in skins with the knees bent to the chest and placed it in a sitting position. They buried men with their bows, arrows, and shields; they buried women with spoons, and with their jewels and ornaments.

# Life in the Late Woodland in Northern Maine

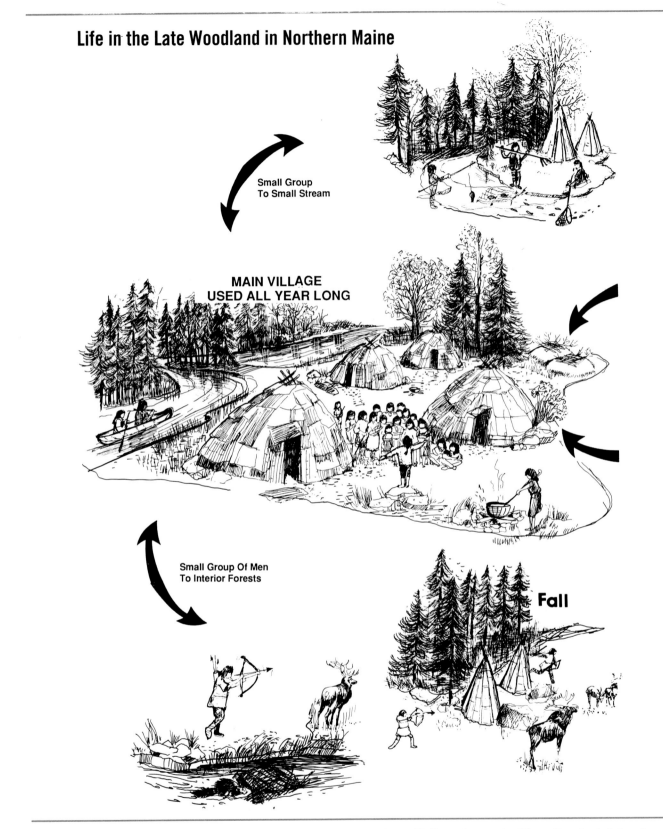

**Small Group To Small Stream**

**MAIN VILLAGE USED ALL YEAR LONG**

**Small Group Of Men To Interior Forests**

**Fall**

Figure 73: The native people of the northern lands followed a way of life closely tied to catching migratory fish in the rivers, fishing and collecting shellfish along the coast, hunting deer and many other animals in the forest, and harvesting many kinds of nuts and berries.

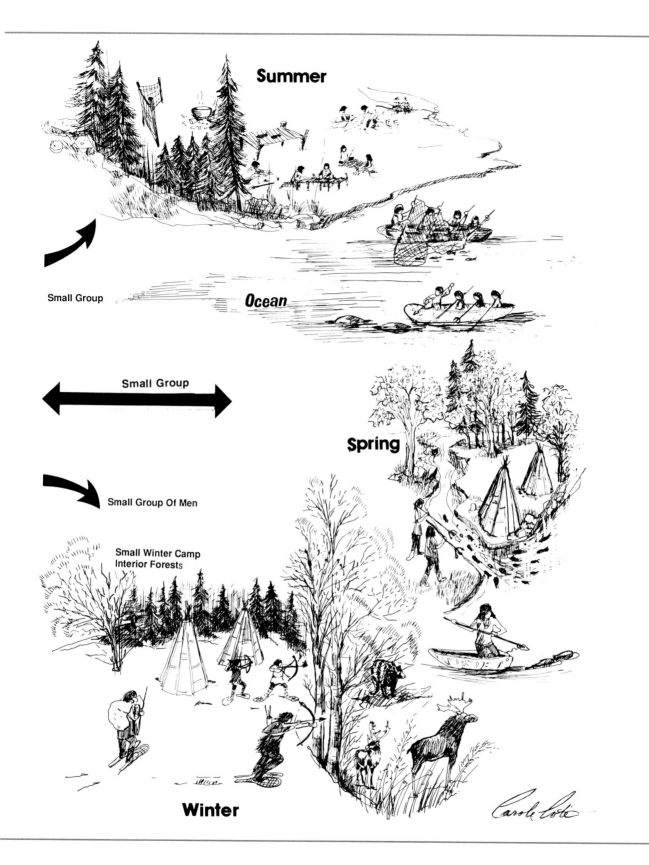

Summer

Ocean

Small Group

Small Group

Small Group Of Men

Spring

Small Winter Camp
Interior Forests

Winter

# Changes Brought by the Europeans

With the arrival of the Europeans, the native peoples of the Northeast soon lost much of their centuries-old heritage. They became caught in the competition among the European countries for both land and furs.

The long-used trade routes among the tribes of the Northeast (see Figure 63) quickly became the main routes for the fur trade. Later, these same routes became roads traveled by the Europeans themselves, and today many highways still follow the ancient routes. For example, the main trade route from Massachusetts Bay into the interior of Massachusetts, the Old Connecticut Path, is now part of Route 20 in Massachusetts. The Pequot Path ran between what are now Providence, New Haven, and New York; it became the Boston Post Road and is now part of U.S. Route 1. An important path through eastern New York and western Massachusetts is still called the Mohawk Trail.

Trading with the Europeans gave the native people many new ways to increase their wealth and their importance among themselves. Trade also was the easiest way to obtain the metal tools and new foods the Europeans brought with them. In many areas, the natives ended up spending more and more time on trapping for trade and less on their usual food gathering activities and crafts. Many natives soon suffered from poor diets.

Former friends became trading competitors. Trapping territories became prized possessions and trespassers were sometimes killed by previously friendly neighbors. Entire tribes also competed over trapping areas; this sometimes led to wars, often between people who were old enemies to begin with. Tribes that could not bring in many furs became poor unless they could find other ways to make themselves valuable to the Europeans, for example as fighters in the colonial wars.

Native peoples abandoned their old crafts as they obtained the more prized European goods. Copper kettles replaced ceramic pots for cooking. Woven fabric took the place of skins. Dutch stockings were used as tobacco pouches. The Europeans brought in white and blue glass beads that looked like the valued shell beads once worn only by chiefs. Now anyone could wear clothes with fancy beadwork, as long as they had goods to trade for the beads. European tools made it much easier to drill the holes to make shell beads, and so shell beads became more plentiful, too.

Some people continued to prefer their older forms of tools and weapons because of the special uses for which they were designed. Yet even in these items, European materials came into use. Metal arrow points and knife blades replaced those made of stone, for example, and many woodcarvings were inlaid with copper or glass.

The native spoken languages also changed. A jargon of mixed French and native words developed among the peoples who lived in close contact with the French. A similar jargon of English and native words arose among the peoples dealing with the English.

Liquor was introduced by the first traders and had a devastating effect on people's health. Most European settlers were forbidden to sell it, but not all of them followed the prohibition. The natives also soon learned how to make liquor themselves, and some became addicted to it. Since every person was important in his or her village's daily work, the introduction of liquor added to the people's hardship.

By far the worst effect of contact was the introduction of European diseases. The human body builds up defenses against the bacteria and viruses which are common in the environment. A virus or bacterium introduced from another part of the world can cause an epidemic, because the natives' bodies have no built-in defenses against it.

Despite their occasional encounters with Europeans during the 1500s, the native people at that time do not seem to have suffered serious epidemics. We do not know why. After 1600, however, larger numbers of Europeans arrived and disaster struck in the form of measles, smallpox, typhus, and other diseases. The natives, having no natural defenses against these plagues, died in thousands. Whole communities disappeared, first on the coast, then inland.

Some tribal groups died out almost completely, while others shrank to pitifully small numbers. Leaders and elders who knew the old ways of living died just as fast as everyone else. Tribal governments broke apart and disputes over leadership and boundaries became common. Many surviving groups joined together into confederacies to protect themselves from their surviving enemies. Some of these confederacies also sought alliances with the different European powers, for further protection.

Some of the native people converted to the English religion, often hoping that this might protect or cure them from the new illnesses. Beginning in 1650, well-meaning colonists led by John Eliot in Massachusetts helped set up "praying towns" for native peoples who joined the Christian religion. The purpose of these

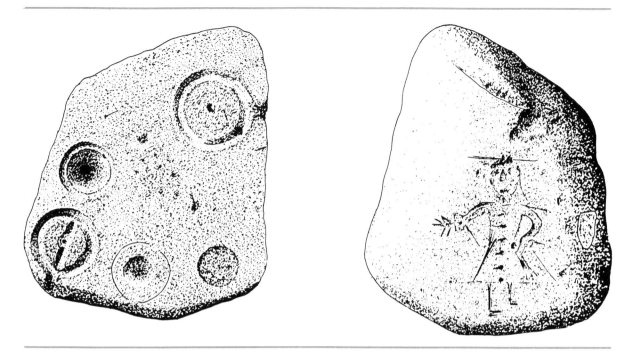

Figure 74: This native-made button mold was found by arcnae-ologists in Lincoln, Massachusetts, in an area once part of the town of Concord where natives who had joined the Christian religion might have lived. (Original drawing by Lisa Anderson in an article by Russell Barber for the Bulletin of the Massachusetts Archaeological Society, reproduced with permission of Russell Barber.)

towns was to educate natives to be good Christian neighbors and loyal British subjects. The first praying town was in Natick. Many of the natives who lived in Natick came originally from the area of Concord, Massachusetts. The number of praying towns increased along the English frontier from 1650 to 1675, when they all ended abruptly during a war known as King Phillip's war, fought by the English with the help of some natives against many New England tribes.

The praying towns were a European experiment in changing the natives' ways of life. It probably had to fail, for many reasons. Each culture really never understood what was important to the other. This created all kinds of conflicts. Furthermore, the native people in the praying towns found it difficult to adapt to English houses and foods. During King Phillip's war, too, some English settlers became suspicious of all natives. They rounded up residents of the praying towns and confined them on Deer Island in Boston Harbor, even though these people had remained loyal to their English neighbors. Their homes and lands at the praying towns also were ransacked by lawless settlers. Later, some Christian natives were forced into mil-

itary service for the English, to help win the war.

The English made some effort to rebuild the praying towns after the war, but this effort lasted only until John Eliot's death in 1690. Then, a new policy began, forcing the natives to live in reservations on their tribal lands, where they could be watched closely by colonial governments.

Although the 1600s mostly were a time of peaceful coexistence between the natives and the growing numbers of Europeans, there also were several wars between the two groups. Native warriors fought in these wars alongside the Europeans, in alliance against other tribes. These alliances, aided by native spies, crushed every native uprising.

Eventually, many people from the southern and eastern tribes fled their lands altogether, to join with tribes living in Canada and around the southern Great Lakes. These people became parts of other cultures, which eventually also were absorbed by the expanding European colonies and by the developing nations of the United States and Canada. Other people, such as the Iroquois tribes in New York and the Passamaquoddy in Maine, found ways to survive and even thrive in the European world.

The Iroquois tribes in fact used their unity to become a powerful group, much sought after as allies by the French and the English. Later, the independent colonists of the region sought out their friendship and help in wars against other native peoples and against the English. The Iroquois eventually became one of the first native peoples to sign a treaty of friendship with the newly formed United States after the American Revolution.

Many native people still live in the Northeast today, descendants of the survivors of the seventeenth century; many still speak their own languages and preserve their own traditions. Throughout the region there still live, to name but a few, Narragansett, Wampanoag, Passamaquoddy, Mohawk, Oneida, Seneca, and Maliseet.

## A Final Word

We have now gone from the earliest ancient times to written accounts of the first contacts between the Europeans and the native peoples of the Northeast. You can learn more about the early years of European contact in. many history books. For now, we must leave the scene. The final chapter explains the role of archaeology in preserving the past before it is lost forever.

# 8

# Archaeology and Conservation

Let us look back for a moment at what we have learned of the past of the Northeast. We have followed the growth, over more than a hundred centuries, of an ever more complex way of life. We have looked at Paleo-Indians who lived in mobile bands; then Archaic bands who moved between small villages and smaller campsites with the seasons; and, finally, Woodland tribal peoples who lived in settled villages. We have learned of the distinctive tools of each time period, and of their preferred settlement locations. We have learned that their numbers, their tools, their ways of finding food, and their social and religious ways also changed over the centuries. And we have learned how the people of each part of our region developed ways of life that set them apart from their neighbors, and so became different societies.

When you stop to think about it, though, what we know is only the smallest fraction of what we would like to know. As you have read this book, you must have stopped at least once, thinking "Why did that happen?" or "How do we know that?" We seem to know only enough to whet our appetite, not to satisfy it.

There truly is a tremendous amount we do not as yet know. Why was it, if archaeologists are correct in their thinking, that no one lived in parts of the Northeast just after the Paleo-Indian period? How did social life change between the Paleo-Indian and Early Archaic periods? Why did the shapes of tools change? Are the Middle Archaic people of the Northeast the direct ancestors of the Indians who first met the European explorers? How ancient are the cultural differences between the different parts of our region? Why didn't the people take to growing crops as quickly as their distant neighbors to the west? Was warfare common before European contact? How did life

change during the first century of contact?

These are but a few of the many questions we could ask. You will have others, but perhaps especially this one: Why do we not yet know the answers?

There are three reasons for our difficulty. First, we have no written records for our region from the centuries before the arrival of the Europeans. People also can pass down their histories through the spoken and remembered words of their elders, but many such histories from before the arrival of the Europeans were lost as slave raids, disease, and warfare devastated the native populations. The written records of the first Europeans to meet the natives of the Northeast tell us only a small fraction of what we would like to know, and they often tell us more about the prejudices and hopes of the Europeans than about the natives. As a result, we frequently must rely on archaeology alone to learn about the first peoples of the Northeast, and this brings us to the second reason for our difficulty.

Archaeology is a very young science. Almost all of the equipment, methods, and theories we have now, developed during only the past few decades, and the methods of archaeology are improving all the time. So many questions are still unanswered because we really have only begun to discover what archaeology can teach us about our region. There will always be new questions to ask as we answer the old ones, of course, but right now is the most exciting and challenging time in the history of archaeology.

The third reason for our difficulty has to do with the destruction of archaeological sites. An archaeological site is an incredibly fragile thing. It is a pattern of tools, refuse, stains, and shaped earth lying in the ground. It is this patterning that gives us our information. Disturb a site, and the pattern is lost forever.

Archaeologists are people trained to keep massive records so that knowledge of what was present at a site can be preserved. Nevertheless, when archaeologists excavate, they destroy the site's pattern, too. What if it is not an archaeologist who disturbs a site? In the Northeast, as we have seen, there are many natural factors that can disturb a site—floods, a rising sea level, tree roots, rodents burrowing. The native people themselves sometimes disturbed sites when they camped on top of an older site and dug new pits for cooking or for their houses. Yet these things are minor next to the destruction caused by modern society.

Almost every harbor town in the Northeast today probably lies on top of at least one ancient site. Most mill towns probably lie on the sites of ancient native fishing villages. Our fields for crops and our suburbs spread out over the farmlands and village sites of the original inhabitants. Our reservoirs submerge the sites where people once camped along streams or lakes. As our own society grows, we destroy the archaeological record. In the Northeast, we have been doing this for over 350 years, since the Pilgrims disturbed a Nauset Indian cemetery on Cape Cod.

We must add to this list of destruction, sadly, one more problem. Since Europeans first recognized the antiquity of the native peoples of America, members of our society have enjoyed collecting objects left by these peoples. Collecting finds from the ground surface, and even digging for relics, has been a hobby for many Americans for over a century. When done carefully and recorded properly, with respect for the dead, and with the finds placed in a museum for others to study, such digging has helped us learn more of the past. But all too often such digging is not done carefully, not recorded, and the finds are kept privately or sold to others. When this happens, we lose all chance to learn.

This, then, is the third reason why there are still so many gaps in our knowledge of our region's past. So much has been destroyed already, that archaeologists must work mostly just to find and save as much as they can of what is left. It is a job far bigger than the few professionals can handle, too. Each and every one of us must help when we can.

How can we help? Archaeologists say that we are all "Stewards of the Past." That means it is up to all of us, in our home towns or at places we visit, to keep a lookout for sites before they are destroyed and to help save ones that are in danger. We must keep a watch to make sure no more is destroyed than is absolutely necessary.

Sometimes the destruction cannot be stopped. It is then up to us to save what we can. A group of people can learn how to excavate and record by attending field schools and, with the advice of a professional archaeologist, they can save information in an emergency. One such group excavated the Neville site in Manchester, New Hampshire, when construction threatened to destroy the site. After the excavations, the site was destroyed, but much information was saved, all of it very important to our knowledge of life during Archaic times.

We can not stop the growth of our own society, but we can guide it, and we can save a lot if there is no other choice. Keep your eyes on places where houses or stores or roads are being built, where fields are being plowed, anywhere where the land is being disturbed. If you find anything, contact an archaeologist, museum, or other office.

Every state has a government office that watches over the state's lands, recording and protecting sites. Many museums and most universities have archaeologists on staff, and every state in the Northeast has an organization of amateur archaeologists, who conduct research alongside the professionals. At the end of this book, in Appendix B, you will find a list of offices and groups who can help you when you find a site, or whom you could join in learning more about your area.

We call the saving of the archaeological record, Conservation. Conservation is not the job just of museums and government offices. They do not have enough time, staff, or money to do it all. Conservation is the responsibility of every one of us. Once any part of the archaeological record is lost, we can never know how much or how little information we have lost. We will know, though, that we no longer have the chance to find out.

You can think of the archaeological record as if it were an ancient book, the only copy left. Already many pages are missing, torn, written over, or faded. Every so often, someone comes along and copies out part of a page, saving its knowledge. Perhaps more often, however, someone or something comes along and tears out a page or more, or tears out a chunk, or writes over a page. Soon the book will be completely ruined. Soon we will lose what little is left.

With a little effort, though, we can save the book, preserve it, and hold it aside. With time we can study it, copy down its knowledge, and learn. So it is with the archaeology of the Northeast. We have much to learn, and we have much still to save.

# Appendix A

## How Archaeology Works

This part of the book briefly describes how archaeologists go about studying the remains of the past. We must keep in mind, though, that the science of archaeology cannot reveal everything about past people. Archaeological sites never preserve everything we would like to study, especially not the thoughts and feelings of people who lived in ways we can only imagine.

### The Goals of Archaeology

Archaeology has two main goals. Archaeologists first try to construct as complete a picture as possible of the way of life of the people who occupied a specific area at a particular time in the past. They then try to understand why a people's way of life changed, or perhaps did not change, over time.

In order to accomplish these goals, archaeologists must collect evidence of the past. This evidence comes from the remains that people leave behind: the remains of their buildings, their garbage, their broken tools, their roads and fields. Look around you. You will see that even your own society leaves evidence of itself everywhere. It is because people always discard and abandon so much, as we go through life, that the archaeologist can learn about the past. Archaeologists use the word "site" for any place where ancient remains occur.

Archaeologists must first discover and then preserve the remains of the past. Frequently, they must chop away trees and vines just to be able to see the ground, or explore underwater to find sunken sites. When a place containing evidence is found, archaeologists must be cautious about doing anything further. Once ancient remains are disturbed, no one can go back to check them again in their original condition. Also, there is always the possibility that more can be learned at a later time, because archaeologists are constantly improving their methods of research.

Thus, even when archaeologists do decide to dig at a site, they usually uncover only a few carefully chosen sections, leaving the rest for future study. During and after the excavations, archaeologists take whatever they have found and carefully record how and where the remains were found. Then they study the materials they have uncovered, to try to form a picture of how and when the people lived. Their final task is to publish a report, so that other people can learn of their discoveries.

Archaeologists look for areas to study, that will help them learn the most about particular times and peoples of the past. Often, too, archaeologists work in areas where construction projects—for highways, bridges, or buildings—may disturb sites. Laws in our country often require that construction projects bring in archaeologists to look for sites before the construction begins to disturb the ground. You may even have heard of archaeologists working with a construction project in your own town.

In order to help them study the remains of the past, archaeologists often work with scientists from numerous other fields. Botanists, for example, study the seeds from ancient food remains; physicists and chemists help measure the age of a sample of charcoal or bone; architects study how ancient buildings were used; and ecologists help in building a picture of the environment in which ancient people lived.

### Finding the Evidence

Archaeologists must search carefully for the remains of peoples' lives from hundreds or even thousands of years ago. These remains often are buried in the ground just where they were last used; it takes only a few years for things left undisturbed on the ground to be completely covered by leaves, dust, soil, or sand. Near volcanoes, volcanic ash or lava can also cover archaeological remains. Eventually, grass and trees may grow on this cover.

Archaeologists studying a particular region use

many clues when looking for ancient remains. For instance, the ground in one location may look different from the surrounding area. There may be small mounds; these could turn out to cover buildings. The grass may be a different color in spots; perhaps something buried there has interfered with the roots. Sometimes the trees in a small area are different from those around them, or the soil is an unusual color, because of what lies below.

In addition to noticing unusual ground conditions, archaeologists may spot broken pieces of pottery, or stones with out-of-the-ordinary shapes. Sometimes these are found by other people, such as farmers, who may recognize what they have found and call in an archaeologist. So, without looking very hard, archaeologists may find themselves with sites to examine.

Most often, though, archaeologists do not rely on accidents of discovery. Instead, they must carefully examine an entire region to identify its sites. Archaeologists call such searches for sites, "surveys." One way to survey an entire region is to look for places where you might expect people to have lived, traveled, or rested. This can be done using maps or aerial photographs that show the features of the land, such as its hills, cliffs, valleys, rivers, streams, ponds, and lakes. A trained person can recognize features that could have attracted human settlement: rivers, shores of ancient lakes, mines, quarries, caves, and rock shelters. Aerial photographs are especially useful for surveys, as they can reveal unusual soil or vegetation patterns that give clues to buried remains. The best way to make a survey, however, is to walk over the entire area. To be sure that they survey an entire region, teams of archaeologists walk over the land in an orderly fashion and keep detailed records of where they have surveyed, how, and when.

## Testing a Site

After archaeologists have surveyed a region, they must decide which, if any, sites to study. Studying a site takes a lot of time and effort, and archaeologists can not afford to spend their time studying every single site in detail. They must spend their time wisely, working at those sites from which they can learn the most, especially sites that might be destroyed by modern construction.

Archaeologists cannot know what lies beneath the ground at a site without excavating, of course, but how can they tell if a site is worth excavating in the first place? Archaeologists carry out "test studies" at sites, to determine which (if any) might be useful for further, detailed study. They choose sites for their test studies using all of the clues they can glean from the surface. As long as there is time to do this, and the owners of the land are willing, archaeologists can gain much information from a test study.

To start the testing, archaeologists first make a map of the site's surface. This map might show where ancient materials have come to the surface, or it might show unusual soils, mounds, or depressions that give clues to buried houses, roadways, or other large ancient constructions. Next, the archaeologists try to learn what kinds of soil layers there are at a site. They do this by digging small, square holes called "test pits," or by removing small, circular columns of soil using special tools. The soil layers at a site give clues about the number and ages of the different groups who may have used the site. Sometimes archaeologists can use special electronic devices to look beneath the ground surface without having to dig any test pits at all. Almost always, they sift the soils from their test holes through fine screening, to look for remains of plants, animals, and tools.

Once a test study is finished, archaeologists must decide whether they should excavate a site further. They have to decide if the information they might gain from additional excavations would be more important than leaving the site alone for studying at some other time. Of course, if the site is going to be destroyed, perhaps by a highway or by natural erosion, they will excavate as much as they can to save whatever knowledge the site may provide. If a site is not threatened, though, archaeologists often find that they already have their hands full finishing reports on other sites, so the excavation of new sites must wait. Also, before excavating at a new site, archaeologists must consider whether there is time enough to complete the job, whether they can get enough people to help, and whether the information from the new site will help answer important questions. Indeed, archaeologists must consider many issues before deciding whether to excavate a new site.

## Excavating a Site

Before excavating a site in detail, archaeologists usually lay out a rectangular grid made with stakes and twine, like a giant graph on the ground. The squares may be any size, but they are usually two meters (about six feet) on a side. A field team prepares a map of the site, showing the location of the grid. Each square in the grid is given a unique label.

The archaeologists in charge then decide which squares should be excavated. A team then begins work on each of these squares. The excavators carefully remove the soil in each square layer by layer, using delicate digging tools, and they draw maps of the soil in each layer. As objects come to light, they are tagged according to their soil layer and square, and their locations are recorded on the maps and in field notes. Even the most careful excavators cannot see everything in the soil as they dig through it, though; all excavators also carefully sift the soils through special screens. They also save soil samples from each layer; these soil samples may contain traces of minerals and microscopic materials, such as pollen, that can help archaeologists with their studies. The excavators keep a record of everything they see, with photographs, sketches, and written notes. When the excavators reach the bottom of the site in each square, they make drawings of the sides of the pit showing the different layers of soils.

Some of the items that can come to light may be bits of charcoal, seeds, or bones; or things that have been made or used by humans for some purpose, such things as tools, pieces of pottery or cloth, or any decorated objects. Some kinds of materials preserve better than others. Objects of stone or metal often last much longer when buried than do objects of bone, wood, or other once-living materials. If the site is in a deep bog, a dry cave, or a very cold place, though, almost all materials can be preserved. Excavations turn up more than just objects to be studied. They can also turn up the remains of buildings, and patterns of unusual soils that show where paths, gardens, and work areas once existed.

## Studying the Evidence

Once the excavations are completed, the archaeologists bring their finds, maps, photographs, and notes back to the museum or laboratory. Here, they begin the much slower task of studying the information and materials from their excavations, layer by layer, to answer questions about the past.

Archaeologists do not work alone in their laboratories. Geologists and chemists examine the minerals in the soils, building materials, and tools. Ceramists study the pottery for the way it was made and used.

Textile specialists study the cloth and the imprints of cloth which are sometimes found on the pottery. Botanists examine the plant remains to find out what plant foods the ancient people ate, and what kinds of wood they used to make tools, build houses, or burn for firewood. Zoologists study the bones and shellfish remains to find out what kinds of animals the people ate or kept as pets, and what kinds of tools they made of bone and shell. The kinds of plant and animal remains found in each layer at a site also provide clues about the environment and how it may have changed.

Archaeologists study the remains of ancient tools to determine how they were used. Archaeologists can tell the most about ancient tools when the tools are found buried right where they were last used. Tools found together with the remains of a butchered animal, for example, were most likely used for butchering the animal. Most often, though, archaeologists find tools buried only where the ancient people threw them out, when the tools broke or became too worn to use anymore. Then, they turn to other clues.

One good clue to how a tool or other object was used is its shape. As we do today in our own society, ancient people made their tools in the shapes that worked best for them. They had different tools to carry out different jobs. A cooking pot, for example, would have a different shape from a jar used for carrying water; a knife for butchering meat would have a different shape from one used to scrape hides; a storage shed would have a different shape from a house; and so forth.

A second way to see how tools were used is from patterns of wear. Archaeologists have found that, when tools are used, they gradually wear down. By looking at the patterns and kinds of wear that show up on different tools, archaeologists can begin to figure out what jobs a tool was used for. Stone knives end up with worn edges, but the pattern of wear will be different if the knife was used on stone or on meat. Cooking pots end up with soot and scraping marks on their outside and scraping and scouring marks on their inside, while other kinds of pots end up with other kinds of wear.

Of course, just as in our own society, ancient people may have used some tools for many different jobs. This makes it harder to figure out how a tool was used—harder, but not impossible. Also, some tools may not be preserved at all. Those made of plant fibers, wood, bone, or shell disintegrate especially easily; without them, archaeologists can put together only an incomplete picture of ancient ways of life.

## Dating the Evidence

To begin making sense of their discoveries from their excavations and from their laboratory studies, archaeologists must determine the age of the remains they study. Layer by layer, and site by site, archaeologists try to figure which remains belong to which time periods of the past.

Our own society can give the age of something by telling us the actual date when something happened, to the day, month, and year. But archaeologists work with the remains of ancient people, most of whom did not keep written records at all, let alone calendars. Instead, archaeologists have developed different ways to tell how old things are, called "relative dating" and "absolute dating." In relative dating, archaeologists determine which sites, soil layers, or artifacts are the oldest, the next-to-oldest, the next-to-next-to-oldest, and so on from oldest to youngest. In absolute dating, archaeologists take things one step further; they determine absolutely how long ago the different sites, soil layers, or artifacts were created. For some research, it is enough to do only relative dating; for other research, it is necessary to go to the extra effort of absolute dating.

Archaeologists have many ways to establish either the relative or the absolute age of ancient remains. We will consider only the most important methods here, especially those that archaeologists use in the Northeast.

The study of soil layering, called "stratigraphy," is the most important method of relative dating. The youngest layers of soil at a site are almost always the ones on top, and the oldest layers are almost always the ones at the bottom. This neat arrangement sometimes can get mixed up, for example by people digging, by animals burrowing, by the uprooting of trees, or by major events such as earthquakes. In most cases, though, archaeologists can determine the relative ages of the materials at a site simply by looking at the order of the soil layers in which the materials were found.

Another method of relative dating is to compare the styles of tools, clothing, and decorations. Archaeologists use the word "style" to mean the special patterns of shape or decoration that different people give to the things they make. Styles always change over time, as peoples' tastes change. You can see this in our own society, too. Even over the past one hundred years, for example, the shapes of the roofs, window trim, and door trim of houses have changed. You can

tell which houses in a town are older than the others, just by their style. You can do this with cars, clothes, dishes, or almost anything else in our own society, and so, too, with the objects made by any other society.

In the Northeast, the shapes of the native peoples' tools, houses, and ornaments, as well as the decorations they placed on materials such as clay pots and pipes, all changed over time. These changes make it possible for archaeologists to tell which sites or materials date to which periods of native history, from oldest (Paleo-Indian) to youngest (Late Woodland). The more we learn of a region's ancient history, the more finely can we determine the relative age of its remains.

Sometimes just the material used to make a tool gives a clue to its relative age. Stone tools were made throughout most of the past, but people in some parts of the world eventually switched to using tools made of refined metals—first bronze, and later iron and steel. Pottery also was invented only a few thousand years ago, in both the Old and New Worlds. The presence of pottery or of different refined metals, therefore, can give a very general clue about the age of a site or layer at a site.

Absolute dating takes a bit more effort than relative dating, because it requires more elaborate laboratory study. The most accurate method of absolute dating is called tree-ring dating or "dendrochronology." This method works only on objects made from tree trunks, such as house posts. If you cut across the trunk of a tree, especially a pine or other evergreen, you will see circles, alternating dark and light. Each pair of dark and light circles shows one year's growth, and the distance from one dark circle to the next shows how much the tree grew during that year. In warm, wet years, the bands between the dark circles are wide; in dry, cold years, they are narrow. The pattern of wide and narrow bands will be the same for all trees growing in an area, wherever the climate was the same across the whole area every year. By matching these patterns, and counting back on a freshly-cut tree, it is possible to figure out a date for each band.

Archaeologists in several parts of the world have matched up the patterns of growth rings to create tree-ring calendars stretching back many hundreds of years. Because the pattern of wide and narrow bands also shows how the climate changed, these tree-ring calendars also give information on the history of climate in their regions. Whenever someone excavates the remains of a tree trunk in one of these regions, scientists can try to match up the patterns of rings on the ancient piece with some portion of the complete tree-ring calendar. If there is a match, then this tells the scientists the absolute age of the ancient piece. Unfortunately, tree-ring dating is not used in the Northeast, but it is used in the American Southwest. The remains of ancient objects made from tree trunks almost never are preserved in the sites of the Northeast, and so archaeologists will probably never have the chance to build a tree-ring calendar for our region.

Many people have heard of the most common method of absolute dating, called "radiocarbon dating." It is not as accurate as dendrochronology, but it can be used more often, and it can be used anywhere in the world. Radiocarbon dating works on anything made from part of a once-living thing, either animal or plant, including charcoal. This is because all living things contain a chemical element called carbon.

When animals breathe out, they exhale carbon dioxide gas. This gas goes into the atmosphere. Living plants then absorb this gas and change it into chemicals called carbohydrates. Animals then eat the plants, or eat other animals that have eaten the plants, digest the carbohydrates to form more carbon dioxide gas, and the cycle starts all over again. The carbon in the atmosphere comes mostly in two different forms. One is a common form, called carbon-12. The other is a radioactive form, called carbon-14, or "radiocarbon." Living plants and animals can use carbon-12 and carbon-14 almost equally well, and so they end up containing both in the same proportions as in the atmosphere.

Carbon-14 has a tendency to change, or "decay," into carbon-12. When an atom of carbon 14 decays into carbon-12, it gives off a tiny amount of radiation, like X-rays. The amount of carbon-14 still present in a piece of material can be determined by measuring the radioactivity given off.

Radiation from the sun hitting our planet's atmosphere continuously turns a few atoms of another element, nitrogen-14, into carbon-14 atoms. So, no matter when a plant or animal lived, it always will have had a steady supply of carbon-14. When the plant or animal dies, however, it stops taking in carbon-14 from the air; instead, the carbon-14 already in the dead body steadily decays into carbon-12, until eventually all of the carbon-14 is gone. Scientists can measure the rate of decay and they have found that, no matter how many atoms there are to start, it always takes about 5730 years for half of the carbon-14 in a dead body to decay into carbon-12, and another 5730 years for half of what is left to decay, and still another 5730 years for half of that to decay, and so on.

Pieces of dead plants and animals often can be found in archaeological sites. For example, the charcoal from an ancient fire was once part of a living tree. Using pieces of these dead plants or animals, scientists can measure how much carbon there is in the piece altogether; then measure the amount of radioactivity given off; and then calculate how much carbon-14 has decayed since that part of the plant or animal was alive. With this knowledge, these scientists can tell the archaeologists the approximate age of the site or of the soil layer from which the piece was excavated. Radiocarbon dating is the most common method for absolute dating in the Northeast.

There are many other methods of absolute dating in archaeology (you may read about these in the books listed in the Bibliography). All of these methods require elaborate laboratory devices developed by scientists from other fields. Today, these other methods almost never get used in the archaeology of the Northeast, but this may change in the future, and new methods may be invented as well.

## Understanding Past Ways of Life

Armed with information about the sites of a region, their materials, and their dating, archaeologists try to put together a picture of how people lived during the different periods in the region's past. The people of each period may have had very different ways of life. Archaeologists therefore must pull together all the information possible for each period, to make sure that they draw as complete a picture for each separate period as possible. As this information grows, too, these pictures of the past may change as they become more accurate.

In order to determine past ways of life, archaeologists must first determine what kinds of activities took place at the different sites used during each period of the past. In ancient times, people often moved around, traveling even great distances to satisfy their needs. Each place they stayed served a special purpose, and in each one they left traces of their having been there. Today, our needs are brought near to us through neighborhood stores. We can live in the same place all the time.

Archaeological sites may be places where people lived, either permanently or only at certain times of the year. For example, fishing camps might have been used only in the spring and hunting camps only in the fall. Other sites may be places where people simply camped out while traveling from one place to another. Still others may be where a single event took place, perhaps the killing and butchering of a large animal. Some sites are ancient quarries, where the stone for the tools was obtained. Still other sites were used only for religious ceremonies. Each kind of site can have different kinds of remains, because people carrying out different activities will leave different materials behind.

In those places where people lived for long stretches of time, archaeologists expect to find the remains of well-built houses, hearths, and storage places. In places where people lived only briefly, or only passed through once, archaeologists expect to find only the remains of temporary shelters and hearths. Sites where the people devoted most of their effort to hunting or fishing, or to collecting a particular plant food, should contain plentiful remains of those animals or plants but few other food remains. Sites where the people devoted their effort to only one kind of activity should contain the remains only of tools used in that activity. The locations of sites—near a river or on a hill, for example—also provide evidence of the activities people may have carried out there. Using these kinds of ideas, archaeologists can begin to form a picture of a past way of life.

Rubbish heaps offer many clues to the lifeways of ancient people. By analyzing the marks on the bones, for example, archaeologists can describe a peoples' hunting or butchering techniques. Plant and animal remains provide information on peoples' diets, the times of year when they hunted different animals, and the local climate.

The sizes of sites provide additional clues. The more time people spent at a site, or the more people who spent time at a site, or both, the larger a site will be. If all sites of a period are small, for example, the people may have lived in small groups or traveled a lot, or both. If some sites are large and others small, then the people may have divided their time between living together in a few large groups and living apart in many smaller ones. The sizes of the sites can not tell us how or why the people came together, or how or why they split themselves up into smaller groups. The sizes of sites only give us clues to follow, using still other kinds of evidence.

Archaeologists can tell if people traded with neighboring or more distant groups by looking at the materials from which their tools were made. Materials that were not native to the region were probably obtained by trade. If people did trade tools and materials, then they may have exchanged ideas with other groups, too.

Archaeologists have gained much knowledge about the past from the study of ancient burials. From them, archaeologists can learn about some of the religious ideas of the ancient peoples. Differences among burials, for example in the kinds of objects placed in the graves, can also give clues to differences in skills and social positions among the members of an ancient society. Archaeologists can also estimate the sizes of ancient populations from the number of bodies buried in cemeteries. We can learn of peoples' diet and health from the condition of their bones and teeth. However, it is extremely important to remember that all burials were probably sacred to the people who left them, and we must treat them with the same respect we would give the burials of people in our own society. Just as you might not wish an archaeologist to dig up the grave of one of your own family's ancestors, other people feel the same way about the graves of their ancestors. Remember that many descendants of the first people of the Northeast are members of our own society today.

Artwork, monuments at ceremonial sites, carvings, and engravings often give archaeologists our only clues to peoples' deepest beliefs about their world. Without written records, we can only guess at what ancient people knew and believed. Yet even very ancient sites throughout the world have yielded evidence that people everywhere have understood much about nature, including astronomy, botany, zoology, and human nature.

Using all the information they have gained from studying the evidence, archaeologists try to arrive at a description of how ancient people lived. This is like putting together a giant picture puzzle, with most of the pieces broken, discolored, or often lost altogether. Yet, through careful, painstaking work, archaeologists can often say a great deal about how ancient people lived and about how their lives changed over time. Trying to explain why people lived as they did, or why their lives changed as they did, takes still further work.

The evidence collected by archaeologists is carefully stored in museums for further research and interpretation. Future archaeologists may want to study the collection. New and improved techniques and equipment may allow us to learn more about the evidence.

Part of the collection may be put on display in a museum, so the general public can gain knowledge and understanding of an ancient people.

Archaeologists are very busy people. While saving sites endangered by construction or erosion, they also carry out studies of materials already excavated from other sites, look for new sites, and publish reports on their previous studies. Many also teach at colleges and universities, or manage collections at museums. If you wish to learn more about archaeology in general or in specific areas of the Northeast, you will find a list of schools, museums, and organizations in Appendix B. Many of these offices and organizations have regular activities, in which you may join. The bibliography at the end of this book also lists some of the many books you may read, to learn more about archaeology in general and about the archaeology of the Northeast in particular. Explore and enjoy!

# Appendix B

## Places to See Archaeological Exhibits and Report Archaeological Finds

Below is a list, arranged by state or province, of some places where you can go to learn more about the archaeology of the Northeast and other parts of your world. The list also tells you of places or people to contact if you find something of archaeological interest yourself. Remember that your first step after making your discovery is to call an expert. It is important not to do any digging or disturbing of a site without the supervision of someone who is trained in archaeology. In state and national parks and forests, in fact, you must not collect or disturb anything that you find at all. The sites on these lands are protected by law; you can help protect them by reporting anything you find to the nearest park or forest office. In addition to the places and people on the list, you may also find that your local library or historical society can direct you to someone who can help you.

### NORTHEASTERN UNITED STATES

### Connecticut

Archaeological Society of Connecticut
P.O. Box 386
Bethlehem, CT 06751
No permanent phone (Check your library)

Connecticut Historical Commission
State Historic Preservation Office
59 South Prospect Street
Hartford, CT 06106
Phone: (203) 566-3005

Institute for American Indian Studies
P.O. Box 260
38 Curtis Road
Washington, CT 06793
Phone: (203) 868-0518
Exhibits, both indoor and outdoor, on New England Native Americans from Paleo through modern times; reconstruction of an Algonkian village; archaeological projects; extensive educational programs; crafts, films, library; school programs

Museum of Natural History
Office of the State Archaeologist
University of Connecticut
Storrs, CT 06268
Phone: (203) 486-5248 or 486-4460
Life-sized wigwam and other Woodland period exhibits; archaeological and anthropological displays; library

Peabody Museum of Natural History
Yale University, Box 6666
170 Whitney Avenue
New Haven, CT 06511
Phone: (203) 436-1710
Exhibits featuring Connecticut Native Americans and archaeology; group programs

Public Archaeology Survey Team
Department of Anthropology
University of Connecticut
Storrs, CT 06268
Phone: (203) 486-4264
Research on Connecticut Native Americans; working with present-day tribes of the area on post-Contact history

Thames Science Center
Gallows Lane
New London, CT 06320
Phone: (203) 442-0391
Exhibit featuring the Thames Valley from the glacial period to modern times

# Maine

Abbe Museum
Sieur du Monts Spring
P.O. Box 286
Bar Harbor, ME 04609
Phone: (207) 288-3519
Exhibits of artifacts from Mt. Desert Island; library, educational programs, including traveling exhibits and slide program

Colonial Pemaquid State Park
Rural Route 2
P.O. Box 117
New Harbor, ME 04550
Phone: (207) 677-2423
Colonial and Native-American collections; archaeology

L. C. Bates Museum
Hinckley Home-School Farm
Hinckley, ME 04944
Phone: (207) 453-7335
Native-American exhibits; classrooms and auditorium

Maine Archaeological Society
P.O. Box 982
Augusta, ME 04332
No permanent phone (Check your library)

Maine State Historic Preservation Commission
55 Capital Street, Station 65
Augusta, ME 04333
Phone: (207) 289-2132

Maine State Museum
Office of the State Archaeologist
State House, Station 83
Augusta, ME 04333
Phone: (207) 564-3032
Display: "12,000 Years in Maine"; educational programs; library

Maine Tribal Unity Museum
Quaker Hill Road
Unity, ME 04988
Phone: (207) 948-3131
500-volume library on American Indians

Nylander Museum
393 Main Street
P.O. Box 1062
Caribou, ME 04736
Phone: (207) 493-4474 or 493-4209

Exhibits on geology and "Native Northeast Americans"; books

Penobscot Nation Museum
Center Street
Indian Island
Old Town, ME 04468
Phone: (207) 827-6545
Artifact exhibits; group programs

University of Maine at Augusta
Department of Anthropology
Augusta, ME 04333
Phone: (207) 622-7131, extension 372

University of Maine at Orono
Department of Anthropology
495 College Avenue
Orono, ME 04469
Phone: (207) 581-1110

University of Southern Maine
Department of Anthropology
Gorham, ME 04038
Phone: (207) 780-5321

# Massachusetts

Aptucxet Trading Post Museum
24 Aptucxet Road
P.O. Box 95
Bourne, MA 02532
Phone: (508) 759-9487
Reconstruction of 1627 trading post

Berkshire Museum
39 South Street
Pittsfield, MA 01201
Phone: (413) 443-7171
Educational programs on Woodland Indians

Blue Hills Interpretive Center
Trailside Museum
1904 Canton Avenue
Milton, MA 02186
Phone: (617) 333-0690
Educational programs; Wampanoag diorama

Boston University
Center for Archaeology
Office of Public Archaeology
Boston, MA 02215
Phone: (617) 353-3415 or 353-3416

Cape Cod Museum of Natural History
Route 6A
Brewster, MA 02631
Phone: (508) 896-3867
School programs; shell-heap exhibit

Cape Cod National Seashore
South Wellfleet, MA 02663
Phone: (508) 349-3785
National Park Service; research in natural history and prehistoric archaeology, research library; publications

Children's Museum
Museum Wharf
300 Congress Street
Boston, MA 02210
Phone: (617) 426-6500
Native American collections; Native American programs; teacher workshops

Concord Museum
200 Lexington Road
Concord, MA 01742
Phone: (508) 369-9763
Exhibits of Concord-area Native American history; artifacts; dioramas; school programs; slides available to rent

Connecticut Valley Historical Museum
194 State Street
Springfield, MA 01103
Phone: (413) 732-3080
Exhibits on Connecticut Valley ethnohistory

Fruitlands Museums
102 Prospect Hill Road
Harvard, MA 01451
Phone: (508) 456-3924
Extensive Native-American collection (some Northeastern); dioramas of scenes from the Woodland period in Massachusetts; large research library

Historical, Natural History, and Library Society of Natick
58 Eliot Street
Natick, MA 01760
Phone: (508) 235-6015
Native American artifacts; John Eliot Bible; Christian Indian displays; site of the Eliot Oak and the Indian Meeting House

Massachusetts Historical Commission
Office of the State Archaeologist
80 Boylston Street
Boston, MA 02116
Phone: (617) 727-8470

Memorial Hall Museum
Pocumtuck Valley Memorial Association
Memorial Street
Deerfield, MA 01342
Phone: (413) 774-7476 or 773-5206
Exhibits covering 10,000 years of history of the Deerfield area, both from the Native American and Anglo-American perspective

National Park Service, North Atlantic Regional Office
Division of Cultural Resources
Regional Archaeologist
15 State Street
Boston, MA 02108
Phone: (617) 223-5054

Peabody Essex Museum
East India Square
Salem, MA 01970
Phone: (508) 745-1876
Exhibits and programs on Native Americans; library

Peabody Museum of Archaeology and Ethnology
Harvard University
11 Divinity Street
Cambridge, MA 02138
Phone: (617) 495-9968
Artifact collections; school programs

Plimoth Plantation, Inc.
Route 3A
Plymouth, MA 02360
Phone: (508) 746-1622
Reconstruction of Wampanoag homesite (including a wetu) and farming, cooking, hunting equipment, and crafts; Native American interpreters; educational programs; school programs

Robbins Museum of Archaeology (Expected to open 1994)
Massachusetts Archaeological Society
Temporary Office: P.O. Box 700
(office temporarily open Wednesdays only, 10 A.M.-3 P.M.)
Middleboro, MA 02346
Phone: (508) 947-9005
Dioramas and artifacts from eastern Massachusetts; library; educational programs

Robert S. Peabody Foundation for Archaeology
Phillips Academy
P.O. Box 71
Andover, MA 01810
Phone: (508) 749-4490
Exhibits on Boylston Street fish weir and other New England sites; Native American artifacts from North America; dioramas; library

Skinner Museum of Mount Holyoke College
35 Woodbridge Street
South Hadley, MA 01075
Phone: (413) 538-2085
Exhibits include Indian artifacts; archaeology; geology

South Shore Natural Science Center
Jacob's Lane
Norwell, MA 02061
Phone: (617) 659-2559
Native American crafts programs for children; archaeology classes and field school

Springfield Museum of Science
236 State Street
Springfield, MA 01103
Phone: (413) 733-1194
Exhibits on New England Native Americans; educational programs

University of Massachusetts, Amherst Campus
Archaeological Services
Blaisdell House
Amherst, MA 01003
Phone: (413) 545-1552

University of Massachusetts, Amherst Campus
Department of Anthropology
Amherst, MA 01003
Phone: (413) 545-2221

University of Massachusetts, Boston Campus
Department of Anthropology
Boston, MA 02125
Phone: (617) 287-5000
Boston Harbor archaeology; community outreach programs

The Vineyard Museum
Dukes County Historical Society
Cooke and School Streets, Box 827
Edgartown, MA 02539
Phone: (508) 627-4441
Artifacts from Martha's Vineyard from Paleo period through Contact; also artifacts from other areas; educational materials for students and teachers; library

Wampanoag Indian Museum
Mashpee, MA 02649
Phone: (508) 477-1536
Wampanoag artifacts

# New Hampshire

Franklin Pierce College
Anthropology Department
Rindge, NH 03461
Phone: (603) 899-5111

Mount Kearsage Indian Museum
Warner, NH 03278
Phone: (603) 456-2600
Native American artifacts from across the country; Native American history, philosophy, lore; 90-minute tour

New Hampshire Archaeological Society
P.O. Box 406
Concord, NH 03302
No permanent phone (Check your library)

New Hampshire State Archaeologist
New Hampshire State Historic Preservation Office
New Hampshire Division of Historic Resources
P.O. Box 2043
Concord, NH 03302-2043
Phone: (603) 271-3483

New Hampshire Historical Society
30 Park Street
Concord, NH 03301
Phone: (603) 225-3381

Philips Exeter Academy
Anthropology Department
Exeter, NH 03833
Phone: (603) 772-4311, ext. # 214
New Hampshire Native American artifacts and exhibits

Plymouth State College
Department of Anthropology
Plymouth, NH 03264
Phone: (603) 253-6386
Programs on New Hampshire Native Americans; educational programs for the New Hampshire school system

University of New Hampshire
Department of Social Sciences
Durham, NH 03824
Phone: (603) 862-2769

White Mountain National Forest
719 Main Street
Laconia, NH 03246
Phone: (603) 528-8721

# New York

American Museum of Natural History
Central Park West at 79th Street
New York, NY 10024
Phone: (212) 769-5100
Native American exhibits; library; traveling exhibits

Buffalo Museum of Science
1020 Humboldt Parkway
Buffalo, NY 14211-1293
Phone: (716) 896-5200
Exhibits in anthropology, geology, natural history; school
loan service

The Cayuga Museum/Case Research Laboratory
203 Genessee Street
Auburn, NY 13021
Phone: (315) 253-8051
Native American artifacts; archaeology; tours; films; educational programs; traveling exhibits

Columbia University
Department of Anthropology
116th Street & Broadway
New York, NY 10027
Phone: (212) 854-1754

Cornell University
Department of Anthropology
Ithaca, NY 14853
Phone: (607) 255-2000

Ganondagan State Historic Site
1488 Victor Holcom Road at Boughton Hill Road
P.O. Box 239
Victor, NY 14564
Phone: (716) 924-5848
Seneca Indian artifacts and European trade items; visitors'
center and trails

Garvies Point Museum
Barry Drive
Glen Cove, NY 11542
Phone: (516) 571-8010
Exhibits on the geology and archaeology of Long Island; dioramas; films; educational programs

Goddard Indian Museum
Bayview Road
P.O. Box 268
Southold, NY 11971
Phone: (516) 765-5577
Native American artifacts; Long Island archaeology; tours;
educational programs; traveling exhibits

The Historical Society of the Tonawanda, Inc.
113 Main Street
Tonawanda, NY 14150-2129
Phone: (716) 694-7406
Native American artifacts; school loan programs

Iroquois Indian Museum
Howes Cave, NY 12049
Phone: (518) 234-8319
Artifacts from Iroquois Indians and their predecessors;
Iroquois art; tours; Indian Festival; slides; library; school
programs

Long Island Culture History Lab and Museum
Suffolk County Archaeological Association
Hoyt Farm Park, New Highway
Commack, NY 11725
(Mail: P.O. Drawer AR, Stony Brook, NY 11790)
Phone: (516) 929-8725
Prehistoric park; Native American artifacts; Long Island
archaeology; educational programs for children and adults;
affiliated with Stony Brook University

Mohawk-Caughnawaga Museum
Route 5, Box 554
Fonda, NY 12068
Phone: (518) 853-3646
Iroquois archaeology and artifacts; excavated Iroquois village

The Museum at Hartwick
Hartwick College
Oneonta, NY 13820
Phone: (607) 431-4480
Artifacts from world-wide prehistoric peoples; Native
American artifacts from the upper Susquehanna River region;
archaeological excavations of the upper-Susquehanna area

Museum of the Hudson Highlands
The Boulevard, Box 181
Cornwall-on-Hudson, NY 12520
Phone: (914) 534-7781
Native American artifacts; geology of the Hudson River
valley; natural history of the area; educational programs

National Museum of the American Indian (opening in 1994)
Alexander Hamilton Custom House
1 Bowling Green
New York, NY 10004
Phone: (not yet available)
Satellite of the main museum which will be in Washington,
D.C.; North and South American Indian art and artifacts

Native American Center for the Living Arts, Inc.
25 Rainbow Boulevard
Niagara Falls, NY 14303

Phone: (716) 284-2427
Native American artifacts and art; research in Native American oral history and culture; educational programs; slides; traveling exhibits

New York State Archaeological Association
Rochester Museum and Science Center
c/o Research Division
657 East Avenue, Box 1480
Rochester, NY 14603-1480
Phone: (716) 271-4320

New York State Museum
Cultural Education Center, Empire State Plaza
Albany, NY 12230
Phone: General Information:
(518) 474-5877
Anthropological Survey:
(518) 474-5813
Life-sized dioramas of the prehistory and history of New York State; geology; natural history; educational programs; school-loan program; archaeological research

New York University
Anthropology Department
70 Washington Square, South
New York, NY 10012
Phone: (212) 998-1212

Rochester Institute of Technology
Anthropology Department
1 Lomb Memorial Drive
Rochester, NY 14623-0887
Phone: (716) 475-2400

Rochester Museum and Science Center
657 East Avenue, Box 1488
Rochester, NY 14603-1480
Phone: (716) 271-4320
Native American artifacts; exhibits on anthropology, archaeology, geology, natural history; tours; films; educational programs

Seneca-Iroquois National Museum
Allegany Indian Reservation
P.O. Box 442
Broad Street Extension
Salamanca, NY 14779
Phone: (716) 945-1738
Iroquois history; archaeology; tours

Six Nations Indian Museum
Rockdale Road
HCR #1, Box 10
Onchiota, NY 12968

Phone: (518) 891-0769
Iroquois artifacts (clothing, wampum, art, pottery); Iroquois culture; diorama of Indian villages of the Iroquois, Delaware, Sioux, and Abenakis; tours; educational programs

State University of New York at Albany
Department of Anthropology
Albany, NY 12222
Phone: (518) 442-4700

State University of New York at Binghamton
Public Archaeology Facility
Binghamton, NY 13902-6002
Phone: (607) 777-4786

State University of New York at Buffalo
Department of Anthropology (includes a museum)
3435 Main Street
Buffalo, NY 14260
Phone: (716) 831-2000

State University of New York at Stony Brook
Department of Anthropology
Stony Brook, NY 11794
Phone: (516) 689-6000

Syracuse University
Department of Anthropology
Syracuse, NY 13244
Phone: (315) 443-3503

Trailside Nature Museum
P.O. Box 236
Cross River, NY 10518
Phone: (914) 763-3993
Natural history; library specializing in Delaware Indians and coastal Algonkian tribes; local geology; Native American artifacts

# Rhode Island

Brown University
Department of Anthropology
Box 1921
Providence, RI 02912
Phone: (401) 863-3251

Haffenreffer Museum of Anthropology
Brown University
Mount Hope Grant
Bristol, RI 02809
Phone: (401) 253-8388
Exhibits on New England Native Americans; reconstructed Woodland village; archaeology exhibits; school programs; traveling programs

Museum of Natural History
Roger Williams Park
Providence, RI 02905
Phone: (401) 785-9450
Programs for school groups on the archaeology and geologic history of Rhode Island, Native American life in southern New England; exhibits of Native American artifacts

Museum of Primitive Culture
604 Kingstown Road
Peace Dale, RI 02883
Phone: (401) 783-5711
Exhibits on archaeology and ethnology; educational programs; traveling exhibits; publication: "Rhode Island's Prehistoric Past"

Narragansett Archaeological Society
No permanent address or phone: call (401) 245-3355 for information

Paumpaquisset Trading Post
Route 2
Charlestown, RI 02813
Phone: (401) 369-8859
Exhibits on New England Native Americans; school programs

Public Archaeology Laboratory, Inc.
387 Lonsdale Avenue
Pawtucket, RI 02860
Phone: (401) 728-8780
Archaeologists; educational programs

Rhode Island College
Department of Anthropology and Geography
Public Archaeology Program
Providence, RI 02908
Phone: (401) 456-9717
Videotapes and traveling exhibits on archaeology

Rhode Island Historical Preservation Commission
150 Benefit Street
Providence, RI 02903
Phone: (401) 277-2678

Rhode Island Historical Society
110 Benevolent Street
Providence, RI 02906
Phone: (401) 331-8575
Archaeological exhibits; teacher's guide to state museums

University of Rhode Island
Department of Sociology and Anthropology
Kingston, RI 02881
Phone: (401) 792-2587

# Vermont

Discovery Museum
51 Park Street
Essex Junction, VT 05452
Phone: (802) 878-8687
Kits and programs on Vermont archaeology and Native Americans

Division for Historic Preservation
Office of State Archaeologist
Pavilion Building
State Street
Montpelier, VT 05602
Phone: (802) 828-3226

Robert Hull Fleming Museum
University of Vermont
Burlington, VT 05405
Phone: (802) 656-0750
Exhibits and loan kits on Native Americans; slides and displays on "The Original Vermonters"

University of Vermont
Department of Anthropology
Williams Science Hall
Burlington, VT 05405
Phone: (802) 656-3884

Vermont Archaeological Society
P.O. Box 663
Burlington, VT 05402
No permanent phone (Check your library)

Vermont Historical Society
Pavilion Building
109 State Street
Montpelier, VT 05602
Phone: (802) 828-2291
Abenaki exhibit; loan kits for schools

## EASTERN CANADA AND THE MARITIMES

# New Brunswick

Centre D'Etudes Acadiennes
University of Moncton
Moncton, NB E1A 3E9
Phone: (506) 858-4083
Research library on Acadian History

Charlotte County Museum
443 Milltown Boulevard

St. Stephen, NB E3L 1J9
Phone: (506) 466-3295
Archaeology exhibit of A.D. 500 Indian settlement in Passamaquoddy Bay area; tours; school loan programs

Miramichi Natural History Museum
149 Wellington Street
Chatham, NB E1N 1L7
Phone: (506) 773-9679
Exhibits on geology; Indian artifacts

New Brunswick Historical Society
120 Union Street
St. John, NB E2L 1A3
Phone: (508) 652-3590

New Brunswick Museum
277 Douglas Avenue
St. John, NB E2K 1E5
Phone: (506) 658-1842
Exhibits on Canadian history, ethnology, geology; traveling exhibits; school programs and kits; lectures; films

Quaco Museum
Quaco Historical and Library Society, Inc.
Main Street
St. Martins, NB E0G 2Z0
Phone: (506) 833-4768
Exhibits include Indian artifacts; educational programs for children

University of New Brunswick
Anthropology Department
P.O. Box 4400
Frederick, NB E3B 5A3
Phone: (506) 453-4864

# Newfoundland

L'Anse Aux Meadows National Historic Park
L'Anse Aux Meadows, NF A0K 2X0
Phone: (709) 623-2608 or 623-2108
Artifacts from the excavation of the site of the first known Viking settlement in North America

Mary March Regional Museum
22 Catherine Street
Grand Falls, NF A2A 2J9
Phone: (709) 489-9331
Collection includes Beothuk and Dorset Indian artifacts

Memorial University of Newfoundland
Archaeology Unit
St. John's, NF A1C 1G3
Phone: (709) 737-3200

Miawipukwik Micmac Museum
Bay d'Espair, NF A0H 1J0
Phone: (709) 882-2470
Traveling exhibits; archaeological research

Newfoundland Historical Society
Colonial Building, Room 15
St. John's, NF A1C 2C9
Phone: (708) 777-3191

Newfoundland Museum
287 Duckworth Street
St. John's, NF A1C 1G9
Phone: (709) 576-2460
Newfoundland archaeology and ethnology collections, including Thule, Dorset, Inuit, Nascapi, Maritime Archaic, Beothuk, and Micmac; research; films; lectures; children's programs

Port aux Choix Interpretation Center
Canadian Parks Service
Great Northern Peninsula
Port au Choix, NF A0K 4C0
Phone: (709) 861-3522
Interpretation Centre features Maritime Archaic Indian culture of area around 2000 B.C.; exhibits of artifacts from burials

Signal Hill National Historic Park
P.O. Box 5879
St. John's, NF A1C 1G3
Phone: (709) 772-5367 or 772-4444
Interpretive Centre covers history of Newfoundland from A.D. 1000 (Vikings) to 1949; tours; school programs

Twillingate Museum
P.O. Box 356
Twillingate, NF A0G 4M0
Phone: (709) 884-5352
Dorset, Inuit, Beothuk Indian artifacts

# Nova Scotia

Beaton Institute of Cape Breton Studies
P.O. Box 5300
Sydney, NS B1P 6J1
Phone: (902) 539-5300
Tapes in Micmac language

Dartmouth Heritage Museum
100 Wyse Road
Dartmouth, NS B3A 1M1
Phone: (902) 464-2300
Exhibits on Micmac Indians

Desbrisay Museum
130 Jubilee Road
Municipal Park
P.O. Box 353
Bridgewater, NS B4V 2W9
Phone: (902) 543-4033
Collection on Micmac Indians and the early Europeans;
educational programs; lectures; tours; films; circulating
exhibits

Halifax Citadel
Cavalier Block
P.O. Box 1480, North Postal Station
Halifax, NS B3K 5H7
Phone: (902) 426-5080 or contact the Nova Scotia Museum
(see below)
Micromac Indian exhibits; Nova Scotia history; archaeology
programs

Historic Resource Research
Parks Canada, Atlantic Region
Upper Water Street
Halifax, NS B3H 1S9
Phone: (902) 426-7515
Archaeology programs

Mic Mac Museum
Rural Route 1
P.O. Box 1003
Pictou, NS B0K 1H0
Phone: (902) 485-4298
Indian artifacts from local burial mounds; 17th-century trade
goods

Mount Saint Vincent University
Anthropology Department
166 Bedford Highway
Halifax, NS B3M 2J6
Phone: (902) 443-4450

Nova Scotia Museum
1747 Summer Street
Halifax, NS B3H 3A6
Phone: (902) 429-4610
Exhibits on natural history, geology, anthropology;
educational programs; lectures; tours; school programs
and kits

Port Royal National Historic Park
P.O. Box 9
Annapolis Royal, NS B0S 1A0
Phone: (902) 532-2397
Reconstruction of French settlement of 1605-1613;
interpretive displays; tours; school programs

St. Mary's University
Department of Anthropology
Robie Street
Halifax, NS B3H 3C3
Phone: (902) 420-5414

# Ontario

Algonquin Museum
Golden Lake Indian Reserve
Highway 60
P.O. Box 28
Golden Lake, ON K0J 1X0
Phone: (613) 625-2027
Collection includes Indian artifacts

Algonquin Park Museum
P.O. Box 219
Whitney, ON K0J 2M0
Phone: (705) 633-5592
Geological and archaeological exhibits

Arkona Lion's Club Indian Art Museum
Smith Street
Arkona, ON N0M 1B0
Phone: (519) 828-3580
Large collection of Indian artifacts; guided tours

Arnprior and District Museum
35 Madawaska Street
Arnprior, ON K7S 1R6
Phone: (613) 623-4902
Exhibits on Indian artifacts, fur trade; guided tours;
children's programs

Brant County Museum
57 Charlotte Street
Brantford, ON N3T 2W6
Phone: (519) 752-2483
Exhibits on Indian history and early pioneer life in the area;
collection of Six-Nations Indian artifacts; lectures; tours;
school programs

Chiefswood Museum
Council House
Six-Nations Reserve
Ohsweken Post Office
Ohsweken, ON N0A 1M0
Phone: (519) 445-2201
Exhibits on Indian history; pre-confederation Indian house

Doon Pioneer Village
Rural Route 2

Kitchener, ON N2G 3W5
Phone: (519) 748-1914
Exhibits include local Indian artifacts; interpreters;
educational programs

Golden Lake Algonquin Museum
Golden Lake Indian Reserve
P.O. Box 28
Golden Lake, ON K0J 1X0
Phone: (613) 625-2027
Exhibits include Algonquin artifacts and early European
artifacts

Haldimand County Museum
Haldimand/Norfolk Regional Museum Board
8 Echo Street
Cayuga, ON N0A 1E0
Phone: (416) 772-5880
Exhibits include Indian artifacts; group tours; workshops

Huron Indian Village
Little Lake Park
P.O. Box 638
Midland, ON L4R 4K9
Phone: (705) 526-8757
Reconstructed Huron Indian village from Late Woodland peri-
od; Indian artifacts and replicas from Contact period; tours;
films

Huronia Museum
Little Lake Park
P.O. Box 638
Midland, ON L4R 4P4
Phone: (705) 526-2844
Pioneer and Indian artifacts; tours; programs for school groups

Joseph Brant Museum
1240 North Shore Boulevard East
Burlington, ON L7S 1C5
Phone: (416) 634-3556
Last home of Captain Joseph Brant, a Mohawk
Indian chief; exhibits include Indian artifacts;
guided tours; lectures; children's educational programs;
school loan service

Kanawa International Museum of Canoes, Kayaks, and
Rowing Craft
School of Physical and Health Education
University of Toronto
320 Huron Street, Room 226
Toronto, ON M5S 1A1
Phone: (705) 489-2644
Exhibits of canoes, kayaks, rowing craft and
equipment for their construction; fur trade canoe tours;
loans

King's College
Anthropology Department
266 Epworth Avenue
London, ON N6A 2M3
Phone: (519) 433-3491

London Regional Children's Museum
21 Wharncliffe Road South
London, ON N6J 4G5
Phone: (519) 434-5726
Programs and exhibits on Inuit, history, ethnology; educa-
tional programs; tours; workshops

McMaster University
Anthropology Department
1280 Main Street, West
Hamilton, ON L8S 4L8
Phone: (416) 525-9140

Museum of Indian Archaeology (London)
Lawson-Jury Building
1600 Attawandaron Road
London, ON N6G 3M6
Phone: (519) 473-1360
Wilfrid Jury Collection of Indian artifacts—40,000 specimens
from southwestern Ontario; interpretive programs; educational programs; courses; archaeological research; reconstruction of "Lawson Prehistoric Indian Village"

Museum of Indian Archaeology and Pioneer Life
Somerville House
University of Western Ontario
London, ON N6A 5B7
Phone: (519) 679-2111
Exhibits on Indian village life

Museum of the North American Indian Travelling College
Rural Route 3
Cornwall Island, ON K6H 5R7
Phone: (613) 932-9452
Exhibits of Iroquois, Ojibwa, and Cree artifacts; tours

National Museum of Man
Metcalfe and McLeod Streets
Ottawa, ON K1A 0M8
Phone: (613) 993-3497
Exhibits on archaeology, ethnology, physical anthropology;
research; guided tours; educational programs; lectures; school
kits; traveling exhibits; numerous publications

Rondeau Park Interpretive Center
Rural Route 1
Morpeth, ON N0P 1X0
Phone: (519) 674-5405
Archaeological collections; films; slides

Royal Ontario Museum
100 Queen's Park
Toronto, ON M5S 2C6
Phone: (416) 586-5549
North American archaeology; ethnology (especially of the American Indian); tours; lectures; films; "Discovery Room"; school programs; traveling exhibits

St. Lawrence Islands National Park: Interpretive Centre
Mallorytown Landing
P.O. Box 469
Rural Route 3
Mallorytown, ON K0E 1R0
Phone: (613) 923-5261
Exhibits on the history of the Thousand Islands region; school programs

Sainte Marie Among the Hurons
Rural Route 1
Midland, ON L4R 4K8
Phone: (705) 526-7838
Reconstruction of Ontario's first European community—both Indian and European houses included

Ska-Nah-Doht Indian Village
Longwoods Road Conservation Area
Rural Route 1
Mount Brydges, ON N0L 1W0
Phone: (519) 264-2420
Reconstruction of sixteen Iroquoian Indian structures; Indian artifacts from southwestern Ontario; displays; theatre; school programs; archaeological excavations

Trent University
Anthropology Department
Peterborough, ON K9J 7B8
Phone: (705) 748-1216

University of Toronto
Anthropology Department
Toronto, ON M5S 1A1
Phone: (416) 978-2011

University of Windsor
Anthropology Department
Windsor, ON N9B 3P4
Phone: (519) 253-4232

Woodland Indian Cultural Education Centre
184 Mohawk Street
P.O. Box 1506
Brantford, ON N3T 5V6
Phone: (519) 759-2650
Woodland Indian artifacts; snowsnake tournament; festival of the Woodland Indian; traveling exhibits; lectures

# Prince Edward Island

Fort Amherst National Historic Park
Rocky Point, PE C0A 1H0
(Mail: c/o Parks Canada, P.O. Box 487, Charlottetown, PE C1A 7L1)
Phone: (902) 892-0203 or 675-2220

Prince Edward Island Museum and Heritage Foundation
2 Kent Street
Charlottetown, PE C1A 1M6
Phone: (902) 892-9127
Archaeology programs; school programs

University of Prince Edward Island
Anthropology Department
550 University Avenue
Charlottetown, PE C1A 4P3
Phone: (902) 892-4121

# Quebec

Archaeological Society of New France
410 Fatima, Les Saules
Quebec, PQ G1P 2C9
Phone: (418) 871-3626
Programs in archaeology

Cartier-Brebeuf National Historic Park
2 rue d'Auteuil
Quebec, PQ G1K 7R3
Phone: (418) 694-4038
Interpretive Centre on the second voyage of Jacques Cartier, the encounter between the Europeans and the Indians in the 16th century; marionnette theatre for children

Concordia University
Anthropology Department
1455 de Maisonneuve
Montreal, PQ H3G 1M8
Phone: (514) 879-5995

Godbout Museum of the American Indian and Inuit
Chemin Pascal Comeau
Godbout, PQ
(Mail: 48 Carillon, Chicoutimi Nord, PQ G7G 3J3)
Phone: (418) 543-3467
Artifacts of American Indians and Inuit; research on American Indians

Historical Society of Marigot, Inc.
440 Chemin de Chambly
Longueuil, PQ J4H 3L7
Phone: (514) 677-4573 or 670-7399
Programs in archaeology

Laval University
Anthropology Department and Museum
Ste. Foy, PQ G1K 7P4
Phone: (418) 656-2131 (University); 656-5030 or 5867
(Museum)
Artifacts and clothing of Inuit

McCord Museum
690 Sherbrooke Street, West
Montreal, PQ H3A 1E9
Phone: (514) 398-7100
Ethnology of Eastern Woodlands; large collection of prehistoric artifacts

McGill University
Anthropology Department
845 Sherbrooke Street West
Montreal, PQ H3A 2T5
Phone: (514) 398-4455

Museum of Baie Comeau
30 rue Carleton
P.O. Box 273
Baie Comeau, PQ G4Z 2H1
Phone: (418) 296-9690
Ethnology; archaeology; Indian artifacts; programs for school groups

Museum of History and Archaeology
Ecole Polyno de La Sarre
C.P.115 avenue Principale
La Sarre, PQ J9Z 2X4
Phone: (514) 333-2512
Prehistoric artifacts of the area

Museum of History and Folklore
Gaspé Bay
Gaspé, PQ G0C 1R0
Phone: (418) 368-5710
Archaeology; ethnology; regional history; traveling exhibits; research in the history and ethnology of the region

Museum of the Lower St. Lawrence
300 rue St. Pièrre
Rivière-du-Loup, PQ G5R 3V3
Phone: (418) 862-7547
Prehistoric archaeology; ethnology; films; lectures

Museum Pièrre Boucher
Pavillion des Ursulines
858 rue Laviolette
Trois-Rivières, PQ G9A 5S3
Phone: (819) 376-4459
Historic and ethnographic objects; Indian artifacts

Museum of Prehistoric Archaeology
University of Quebec
3351 boulevard des Forges
Trois Rivières, PQ G9H 5A5
Phone: (819) 376-5229
Exhibit: "Evolution of Man"; French and Indian archaeology; dioramas; demonstrations of the manufacture of prehistoric tools; educational activities

Museum of Saguenay-Lac Saint-Jean
534 rue Jacques Cartier East, Suite 30
Chicoutimi, PQ G7H 5K3
Phone: (418) 545-9400
Prehistoric archaeology; Indian and Inuit artifacts

National Archives of Quebec
Regional Centre of the North Shore
500 boulevard Laure
Sept-Îsles, PQ J4R 1X7
Phone: (418) 962-3434

Odonak Museum
Abenaki Indian Reserve
Odonak, PQ J0G 1H0
Phone: (514) 568-2600
Exhibits on the lifeways of the Abenakis and other Indian tribes

Pointe-à-Callière
Montreal Museum of Archaeology and History
350 Place Royale
Old Montreal, PQ H2Y 3Y5
Phone: (514) 872-9150
Exhibits cover 600 years of Montreal History; exhibit: "From Wampum to Credit Cards"; children's discovery programs in archaeology

Redpath Museum
859 Sherbrooke Street West
Montreal, PQ H3A 2K6
Phone: (514) 398-4087
Open for research use only
Paleontology; paleobotany; ethnology; geology; anthropology; archaeology

Regional Museum of the Upper Richelieu
182 Jacques-Cartier North
Saint-Jean-sur Richelieu, PQ J3B 7W3
Phone: (418) 347-0649
Indian artifacts from the Richelieu River region

Sept-Îsles Museum
380 Dequen
Sept-Îsles, PQ G4R 2O8

Phone: (418) 968-2070 or 968-1609
Exhibits on the archaeology of the north shore of the St. Lawrence River; ethnology of the region; culture of the Montagnais; traveling exhibits; reconstruction of an Indian encampment

Sherbrooke Seminary Museum
195 Marquette Street
Sherbrooke, PQ J1H 1L6
Phone: (819) 564-3200
Natural sciences; ethnology; archaeology; guides; audio-visual presentations

University of Montreal
Anthropology Department Laboratory Museum
3150 rue Jean-Brillant
P.O. Box 6128
Montreal, PQ H3C 3J7
Phone: (514) 343-6577
Ethnology

# Illustration Credits

All figures not otherwise credited were prepared by the authors. The maps in Figures 1, 2, 8, 10, 16, 17, 23, 25, 39, 50, 62, 63c, and 64 were drawn by Betsy Pillsbury. Figures 3, 4, 6b, 7a, 7c, 9, 11, 13, 20, 27, 28, 35, 68, 69, and 73, and the animals in Figure 17 are by Carole Cote; the drawings in the Time Line are details from these figures. Figure 5, most of Figure 14, and Figures 19, 21, 26a, 34a, 37, 41, 42b, 48, 53, 57, 58, and 70b are by William Fowler and are from the Bulletin of the Massachusetts Archaeological Society, reproduced with the permission of the Society. The specific references for Mr. Fowler's drawings appear in the list below. The hammerstone in Figure 14 was drawn by William Fowler for the 1976 Artifact Handbook published by the Massachusetts Archaeological Society (see bibliography), reproduced with the permission of the Society. Figure 18 was prepared for the Massachusetts Archaeological Society by John Seakwood, reproduced with the permission of the Society. Figure 42b is by William J. Howes, from the Bulletin of the Massachusetts Archaeological Society, Vol. 15 (October 1954):31, reproduced with the permission of the Society. Figure 74 is by Lisa Anderson in an article written by Dr. Russell Barber for the Bulletin of the Massachusetts Archaeological Society, Vol. 45 (1984, no. 2):49, and is reproduced with the permission of Dr. Barber as well. Figures 6a, 34b-d, and 60b appeared in Blancke and Robinson (1985); Figure 34c is reproduced with the permission of Charles W. Dee, and the others are reproduced with the permission of the Concord Museum, Concord, Massachusetts. Figures 7b, 33b, 54, and 70a are photographs of paintings at the Royal Ontario Museum, reproduced with permission. Figure 12 was provided by Dr. Richard M. Gramly, and it is also used as the Frontispiece. Figures 15, 24, 26b, 29, 30, 31, 32, 36, 38, 43, 44, 46, 47, 51, 52, 56, 60a, 61, 66, and 72 are courtesy of the New York State Museum. Figures 22, 49, and 71 are from the University of New Hampshire Media Service, reproduced with permission. Figure 33a is courtesy of The New England. Figure 40 is a composite of drawings by Dr. Walton C. Galinat, reproduced with his verbal permission and that of American Society of Agronomy, Inc; Crop Science Society of America, Inc; and Soil Science Society of America, Inc. Figure 45 was provided by Dr. Dean R. Snow, and is reproduced with permission of Dr. Snow and the photographer, Louise Basa. Figure 55 is from the Buffalo Museum of Science, reproduced with permission. Figure 59 is from The Plimoth Plantation, Inc., reproduced with permission. Figures 63a and 63b are from *Indian New England Before the Mayflower* by Howard S. Russell, reproduced with the permission of University Press of New England, © 1980 by Trustees of Dartmouth College, and of his family. Figure 65 is from the Peabody Museum of Archaeology and Ethnology, Harvard University, reproduced with permission. Figure 67 is from a sixteenth-century map titled "Belgii Novi, Angliae Novae, et partes Virginiae novissima delineatio," drawn in Amsterdam by Joannis Janssonius, reprinted with the permission of the Harvard Map Collection, Harvard University Library, Cambridge, Massachusetts.

Volume and Page References for Drawings by William Fowler Reproduced from the Bulletin of the Massachusetts Archaeological Society:

Figure 5      34 (October 1972-January 1973): 3.
Figure 14     11 (July 1950): 94(bone tools);
              25 (October 1963): 5(knife), 7(drills),
                  20(scrapers), 27(graver);
              34 (April-July 1973): 3(abrader)
Figure 19     25 (October 1963): 19(shaft abrader)
              25 (April-July 1964): 61(harpoon)
              28 (October 1966): 3(adz, celt, drill)
              29 (April-July 1968): 55(bifurcated point, oval
                  atlatl weight, gouge)
              34 (April-July 1973): 3(notchers, roughing
                  knife, shaft scraper).

Figure 21    23 (April-July 1962): 36(Middle Level, scraper;
                     Highest Level, scraper), 37(Middle Level, knife);
             25 (October 1963): 3(Lowest Level, Neville point; Middle
                     Level, Stark point; Highest Level, Merrimack point),
                     7(Lowest Level, perforator), 10(Middle Level, axe),
                     16(Middle Level, atlatl weight; Highest Level, atlatl
                     weight)
             29 (April-July 1968): 55(Middle Level, perforator;
                     Highest Level, ulu);
             34 (April-July 1973): 3(Middle Level, shaft abrader).
Figure 26a   33 (April-July 1972): 13.
Figure 34a   11 (July 1950): 94(bone fish hook, points);
             25 (October 1963): 10(grooved axe), 16(atlatl  weight);
             25 (April-July 1964): 61(small stone triangles);
             28 (October 1966): 3(paint cup and pestle);
             28 (April-July 1967): 48(plummet, graphite);
             29 (April-July 1968): 47(grooved gouge), 55(ulu);
             31 (October 1969-January 1970): 6(drills),
                     20(mortar and pestle);
             33 (October 1971-January 1972): 14(bone
                     needles), 18(beaver tooth, bone handle);
             33 (April-July 1972): 7(strike-a-light);
             34 (April-July 1973): 3(roughing knife,
                     abrader, notcher).
Figure 37    34 (April-July 1973): 18.
Figure 41    27 (April-July 1966): 52.
Figure 42a   27 (April-July 1966): 57.
Figure 48    33 (October 1971-January 1972): 15.
Figure 53    35 (October 1973-January 1974): 29, 30.
Figure 57    27 (April-July 1966): 60.
Figure 58a   34 (October 1972-January 1973): 23.
Figure 58b   27 (April-July 1966): 65.
Figure 70b   34 (April-July 1973): 9.

# Bibliography

## Suggested Further Reading

Below is a list of books and articles listed in the Bibliography which the reader will find especially useful if more information on a particular topic or time period is desired:

A. Books covering all time periods:

Haviland, 1981; Horwood, 1985; Jennings, J., 1978; Josephy, 1968; Ritchie, 1969 and 1980; Snow, 1976 and 1980; Trigger, ed., 1978; Tuck, 1976.

B. Books or articles which cover specific time periods:

Chapter 1 *The Ice Ages and the First Americans*: Canby, 1979; Fagan, 1987 and 1991; Fladmark, 1986; Jorgensen, 1971; Strahler, 1966; Teller, 1987.

Chapter 2 *The Last Ice Age and the First Peoples of the Northeast*: Borns, 1985; Brigham-Grette, 1988; Fitting, 1978a; Funk, 1978; Larson, 1982; MacDonald, 1968 (Debert site); Newman, 1977; Salwen, 1978; Skehan, 1979.

Chapter 3 *The Early and Middle Archaic Periods*: Dincauze, 1976 (Neville site); Robbins, 1967 (Titicut site); Salwen, 1978.

Chapter 4 *The Late Archaic Period*: Ritchie, 1980, pp. 36-79 (Lamoka Lake site); Robbins, 1980 (Wapanucket site); Salwen, 1978.

Chapter 5 *The Early and Middle Woodland Periods*: Fitting, 1978b; Tuck, 1978a.

Chapter 6 *The Late Woodland Period*: Snow, 1978; Tuck, 1978a and 1978b.

Chapter 7 *European Contact*: Brasser, 1978a; Cronon, 1983; Deetz, 1977; Erickson, 1978; Goddard, 1978; Morrison, 1971; Russell, 1980; Salisbury, 1982; Tooker, 1978; Vaughn, 1965.

Appendix A: Aiken, 1990; Hole and Heizer, 1977; Massachusetts Archaeological Society, 1991; Mitchell, 1984; Willey, 1966.

C. Resource guides for teachers:

American Friends Service Committee, 1989; Krass and O'Connell, 1992; Robinson, 1988.

## Bibliography

Aitken, Martin J.
1990 *Science-based Dating in Archæology*. New York: Longman.
American Friends Service Committee
1989 *The Wabanakis of Maine and the Maritimes*. Bath, Maine: Maine Indian Program.
Bakeless, John
1961 *The Eyes of Discovery*. New York: Dover.
Barber, Russell
1984 Treasures in the Peabody's Basement. *Bulletin of the Massachusetts Archæological Society*, 45(2):49.
Bjorkland, Karna L.
1969 *The Indians of Northeastern America*. New York: Dodd, Mead & Company.
Blancke, Shirley and Barbara Robinson
1985 *From Musketaquid to Concord*. Concord, Massachusetts: Concord Antiquarian Museum.
Bordaz, Jacques
1970 *Tools of the Old and New Stone Age*. Garden City, New York: Natural History Press.
Borns, Harold W., Jr., Pierre La Sable, and Woodrow B. Thompson, editors
1985 *Late Pleistocene History of New England and Adjacent Quebec*. Geological Survey of America, Special Paper No. 197. Boulder, Colorado.
Borraclough, Geoffrey, editor
1979 *The Times Atlas of World History*. Maplewood, New Jersey: Hammond, Inc.
Bradford, William
1898 *History of Plimoth Plantation*. Printed from the original manuscript under the direction of the Secretary of the Commonwealth, by order of the General Court of Massachusetts. Boston: Wright and Potter Printing Company.
Brasser, Ted J.
1978a Early Indian-European Contact. In Bruce G. Trigger, editor, *Handbook of North American Indians, Volume 15, Northeast*, pp. 78-88. Washington, D.C.: Smithsonian Institution Press.

1978b Mahican. In Bruce G. Trigger, editor, *Handbook of North American Indians, Volume 15, Northeast*, pp. 198-212. Washington, D.C.: Smithsonian Institution Press.

Brennan, Louis A.
1975 *Artifacts of Prehistoric America*. Harrisburg, Pennsylvania: Stackpole Books.

Brigham-Grette, Julie, editor
1988 *Field Trip Guidebook*. AMQUA Contribution No. 63. Department of Geology and Geography, University of Massachusetts, Amherst.

Canby, Thomas Y.
1979 The Search for the First Americans. *The National Geographic*, 156 (September, no. 3 ): 330-363.

Champlain, Samuel
1907 *Voyages of Samuel de Champlain, 1604-1618*, edited by W. L. Grant for *Original Narratives of Early American History*. New York: Charles Scribner's Sons.

Coon, Nelson
1969 *Using Wayside Plants*. New York: Hearthside Press, Inc.

Cronon, William
1983 *Changes in the Land: Indians, Colonists, and the Ecology of New England*. New York: Hill and Wang.

Crowl, George H. and Robert Stuckenrath, Jr.
1977 Geological Setting of the Shawnee-Minisink Paleo-Indian Archaeological Site. *Annals of the New York Academy of Sciences*, 288:218-22.

Curran, MaryLou and Dena F. Dincauze
1977 Paleoindians and Paleo Lakes: New Data from the Connecticut Drainage. *Annals of the New York Academy of Sciences*, 288:333-348.

Deetz, James
1977 *In Small Things Forgotten: The Archæology of Early American Life*. Garden City, New York: Anchor Books/Doubleday.

Diamond, Jared
1992 The Arrow of Disease. *Discover Magazine*, October:64-73.

Dincauze, Dena F.
1971 An Archaic Sequence for Southern New England. *American Antiquity*, 36:194-198.

1972 The Atlantic Phase: A Late Archaic Culture in Massachusetts. *Man in the Northeast*, 4:40-61 and Plates VI, VII, VIII.

1973 Prehistoric Occupation of the Charles River Estuary: A Paleographic Study. *Bulletin of the Archæological Society of Connecticut*, 38:25- 39.

1974 An Introduction to Archæology in the Greater Boston Area. *Archæology of Eastern North America*, 2(1):39-67.

1976 *The Neville Site: 8000 Years at Amoskeag, Manchester, New Hampshire*. Peabody Museum Monographs, No. 4. Cambridge, Massachusetts: Harvard University, Peabody Museum of Archaeology and Ethnology.

1979 The Archaeology of Northeastern North America. A course given at the University of Massachusetts, Amherst, Massachusetts.

Dincauze, Dena F. and Mitchell T. Mulholland
1977 Early and Middle Archaic Site Distributions and Habitats in Southern New England. *Annals of the New York Academy of Sciences*, 288:439-456.

Erickson, Vincent O.
1978 Maliseet-Passamaquoddy. In Bruce G. Trigger, editor, *Handbook of North American Indians, Volume 15, Northeast*, pp. 123-136. Washington, D.C.: Smithsonian Institution Press.

Fagan, Brian M.
1987 *The Great Journey*. London: Thames and Hudson.
1991 *Ancient North America*. London: Thames and Hudson.

Fitting, James E.
1978a Prehistory in the Northeast. In Bruce G. Trigger, editor, *Handbook of North American Indians, Volume 15, Northeast*, pp. 14-15. Washington, D.C.: Smithsonian Institution Press.

1978b Regional Cultural Development 300 B.C. to A.D. 1000. In Bruce G. Trigger, editor, *Handbook of North American Indians, Volume 15, Northeast*, pp. 44-57. Washington, D.C.: Smithsonian Institution Press.

Fladmark, Knut R.
1986 Getting One's Berings. *Natural History Magazine*, November:8-18.

Ford, Richard I.
1974 Northeastern Archaeology: Past and Future Directions. *Annual Review of Anthropology*, 3:385-413.

Funk, Robert E.
1977 Early Cultures in the Hudson Drainage Basin. *Annals of the New York Academy of Sciences*, 288:316-332.

1978 Post-Pleistocene Adaptations. In Bruce G. Trigger, editor, *Handbook of North American Indians, Volume 15, Northeast*, pp. 16-27. Washington, D.C.: Smithsonian Institution Press.

Galinat, Walton C.
1988 The Origin of Corn. In G. F. Sprague and J. W. Dudley, editors, *Corn and Corn Improvement, Third Edition, ASA Monograph no. 18*, pp. 1-31. Madison, WI: American Society of Agronomy, Inc.; Crop Science Society of America, Inc.; and Soil Science Society of America, Inc.

Goddard, Ives

    1978   Eastern Algonquian Languages. In Bruce G. Trigger, editor, *Handbook of American Indians, Volume 15, Northeast*, pp. 70-77. Washington, D.C.: Smithsonian Institution Press.

Gramly, Richard M.

    1982   *The Vail Site: A Paleo-Indian Encampment in Maine*. Bulletin of the Buffalo Society of Natural Sciences, Vol. 30. Buffalo: The Buffalo Society of Natural Sciences.

Griffin, James B.

    1967   Eastern North American Archaeology: A Summary. *Science*, 156(No. 3772):175-191.

Haviland, William A. and Marjory W. Power

    1981   *The Original Vermonters*. Hanover, New Hampshire: University Press of New England.

Hayes, Charles F., III, general editor

    1980   *Proceedings of 1979 Iroquois Pottery Conference*. Rochester Museum and Science Center, Research Records, No. 13. Rochester, New York.

Hole, Frank and Robert F. Heizer

    1977   *Prehistoric Archæology*. New York: Holt, Rinehart and Winston.

Horwood, Joan

    1985   *Viking Discovery: L'Anse Aux Meadows*. St. John's, Newfoundland: Jesperson Press.

Ingstad, Helga

    1971   Norse sites at L'Anse aux Meadow. In Geoffrey Ashe, editor, *The Quest for America*, pp. 96-115 and 175-199. New York: Praeger Publishers.

Jennings, Francis

    1984   *The Ambiguous Iroquois Empire*. New York: W. W. Norton & Co.

Jennings, Jesse D., editor

    1978   *Ancient Native Americans*. San Francisco: W. H. Freeman and Co.

Johnson, Frederick, et al.

    1942   *The Boylston Street Fishweir*. Papers of the Robert S. Peabody Foundation for Archaeology, Vol. 2. Andover, Massachusetts.

Johnson, Frederick, editor

    1949   *The Boylston Street Fishweir II*. Papers for the Robert S. Peabody Foundation for Archaeology, Vol. 4(1). Andover, Massachusetts.

Jorgensen, Neil

    1971   *A Guide to New England's Landscape*. Barre, Massachusetts: Barre Publishers.

Josephy, Alvin M., Jr.

    1968   *The Indian Heritage of America*. New York: Alfred A. Knopf.

Kagan, Hilde Heun, editor

    1966   *The American Heritage Pictorial Atlas of United States History*. New York: American Heritage Publishing Company, Inc.

Kammen, Michael G.

    1975   *Colonial New York*. New York: Charles Scribner's Sons.

Koteff, Carl

    1963   Glacial Lakes Near Concord, Massachusetts, Article 96 in *U.S. Geological Survey Professional Paper 475-C*, pp. C142-C144.

    1964   *Surficial Geology of the Concord Quadrangle, Mass., Middlesex County*. GQ-331, Department of the Interior, U.S. Geological Survey.

Kraft, Herbert C.

    1977   Paleoindians in New Jersey. *Annals of the New York Academy of Sciences*, 288:264-281.

Krass, Dorothy Schlottauer and Barry O'Connell, editors

    1992   *Native Peoples and Museums in the Connecticut River Valley*. Northampton, Massachusetts: Historic Northampton.

Larson, Grahame J. and Byron D. Stone, editors

    1982   *Late Wisconsinan Glaciation of New England*. Dubuque, Iowa: Kendall/Hunt Publishing Co.

MacDonald, George F.

    1968   *Debert: A Paleo-Indian Site in Central Nova Scotia*. National Museum of Canada, Anthropological Paper No. 16. Ottawa.

Martin, P. S. and H. E. Wright, Jr.

    1967   *Pleistocene Extinctions*. New Haven: Yale University Press.

Massachusetts Archaeological Society

    1976   *A Handbook of Indian Artifacts from Southern New England*. Attleboro, Massachusetts: Massachusetts Archaeological Society.

    1991   *A Handbook of Indian Artifacts from Southern New England*, revised by Curtiss Hoffman. Middleborough, Massachusetts: Massachusetts Archaeological Society.

McHargue, Georgess, and Michael Roberts

    1977   *A Field Guide to Conservation Archæology in North America*. New York: J. B. Lipincott.

Mitchell, John Hanson

    1984   *Ceremonial Time: Fifteen Thousand Years on One Square Mile*. New York: Warren Books.

Morgan, Lewis Henry

    1851   *League of the Ho-dé-no-sau-nee or Iroquois*. Reprinted, 1962, facsimile edition with an introduction by W. N. Fenton. New York: Corinth Books.

Morrison, Samuel Eliot

    1971   *The European Discovery of America*. New York: Oxford University Press.

Newman, W. S. and Bert Salwen, editors

    1977   Amerinds and their Paleoenvironments in Northeastern North America. *Annals of the New York Academy of Sciences*, Vol. 288.

Norman, Charles
1968 *Discoverers of America.* New York: Thomas Y. Crowell.

Richardson, Joan
1981 *Wild Edible Plants of New England.* Yarmouth, Maine: DeLarme Publishing Company.

Ritchie, William A.
1969 *The Archæology of Martha's Vineyard.* Garden City, New York: Natural History Press.
1980 *The Archæology of New York State, Revised Edition.* Harrison, New York: Harbor Hill Books.

Ritchie, William A., and Robert E. Funk
1973 *Aboriginal Settlement Patterns in the Northeast.* New York State Museum, Memoir No. 20. Albany.

Ritchie, William A. and Richard S. MacNeish
1949 The Pre-Iroquoian Pottery of New York State. *American Antiquity,* 2:97-124.

Robbins, Maurice
1967 The Titicut Site. *Bulletin of the Massachusetts Archæological Society,* 28(3+4):1-10.
1980 *Wapanucket, An Archæological Report.* Attleboro, Massachusetts: Trustees of the Massachusetts Archaeological Society.

Robinson, Barbara
1988 *The Native American Sourcebook: A Teacher's Resource on New England Native Peoples.* Concord, Massachusetts: Concord Antiquarian Museum.

Russell, Howard S.
1980 *Indian New England Before the Mayflower.* Hanover, New Hampshire: University Press of New England.

Salisbury, Neal
1982 *Manitou and Providence: Indians, Europeans, and the Making of New England, 1500-1643.* New York: Oxford University Press.

Salwen, Bert
1978 Indians of Southern New England and Long Island: Early Period. In Bruce G. Trigger, editor, *Handbook of North American Indians, Volume 15, Northeast,* pp. 160-176. Washington, D.C.: Smithsonian Institution Press.

Sanger, David, R. B. Davis, Robert G. McKay and Harold W. Borns, Jr.
1977 The Hirundo Archaeological Project—An Inter-disciplinary Approach to Central Maine Prehistory. *Annals of the New York Academy of Sciences,* 288:457-471.

Scheele, William E.
1963 *The Earliest Americans.* Cleveland: World Publishing Co.

Shattuck, Lemuel
1835 *A History of the Town of Concord.* Boston: Russell, Odiarne & Company.

Shepherd, William R.
1964 *Historical Atlas, Ninth Edition.* New York: Barnes and Noble, Inc.

Skehan, James W., S.J.
1979 *Puddingstone, Drumlins and Ancient Volcanoes, A Geologic Field Guide Along Historic Trails of Boston.* Dedham, Massachusetts: WesStone Press.

Snow, Dean R.
1976 *The Archæology of North America.* New York: Viking Press.
1978 Late Prehistory of the East Coast. In Bruce G. Trigger, editor, *Handbook of North American Indians, Volume 15, Northeast,* pp. 58-69. Washington, D.C.: Smithsonian Institution Press.
1980 *The Archæology of New England.* New York: Academic Press.

Strahler, Arthur N.
1966 *A Geologist's View of Cape Cod.* Garden City, New York: Natural History Press.

Teller, James T.
1987 Glacial Lakes and the Southern Margin of the Laurentide Ice Sheet. In *The Geology of North America, Vol. K-3, North America and Adjacent Oceans During the Last Glaciation,* pp. 39-52. Geological Society of America.

Thomas, David H.
1974 *Predicting the Past.* New York: Holt, Rinehart and Winston, Inc.

Thompson, John H., editor
1966 *Geography of New York State.* Syracuse, New York: Syracuse University Press.

Tooker, Elisabeth
1978 The League of the Iroquois. In Bruce G. Trigger, editor, *Handbook of American Indians, Volume 15, Northeast,* pp. 418-441. Washington, D.C.: Smithsonian Institution Press.

Trigger, Bruce G.
1990 Plate 33. In R. Cole Harris, editor, *Historical Atlas of Canada, Vol. I.* Toronto: University of Toronto Press.

Trigger, Bruce G., editor
1978 *Handbook of North American Indians, Volume 15, Northeast.* Washington, D.C.: Smitsonian Institution Press.

Tuck, James A.
1970 An Archaic Indian Cemetery in Newfoundland. *Scientific American,* 222(6):112-121.
1976 *Newfoundland and Labrador Prehistory.* Toronto: Van Nostrand Reinhold, Ltd.
1978a Regional Cultural Development 3000 to 300 B.C. In Bruce G. Trigger, editor, *Handbook of North American Indians, Volume 15, Northeast,* pp. 28-43. Washington, D.C.: Smith-

sonian Institution Press.

1978b   Northern Iroquoian Prehistory. In Bruce G.
        Trigger, editor, *Handbook of North American
        Indians, Volume 15, Northeast*, pp. 322-333.
        Washington, D.C.: Smithsonian Institution
        Press.

Vaughan, Alden T.

1965    *New England Frontier*. Boston: Little, Brown &
        Company.

Vogel, Virgil

1970    *American Indian Medicine*. Norman, Okla-
        homa: University of Oklahoma Press.

Willey, Gordon R.

1966    *An Introduction to American Archæology,
        Volume I: North and Middle America*. Engle-
        wood Cliffs, New Jersey: Prentice Hall.

Wood, William

1634    *New England Prospect*. Reprinted 1977, Alden
        T. Vaughan, editor. Amherst: University of
        Massachusetts.

# Index

Dugout canoes. *See* Canoes, dugout.
Dutch, the. *See* European explorers; European settlements in the Northeast.

Early Archaic period, 29-32;
　base camp in, 32;
　life in, 31, 32;
　sites, **30** (map), 31-32;
　stone tools in, **33** (illustr.).
Early Woodland period, 62-67;
　camps, 62;
　life in, 65-66;
　sites, **61** (map), 62, 66, 68; Boucher, Vermont, 68; Scaccia, New York (Meadowood), 66.
Ecologists. *See* Scientists, who work with archaeologists.
Eels, 98. *See also* Fish, migratory.
Effigy. *See also* Religious beliefs.
　bird in flight plummet, **42** (illustr.);
　pipes, **81** (illustr.);
　whale, **43** (illustr.).
Eliot, John, 102-103.
Elk, **31** (map), 43, 98. *See also* Food, Lake Forest Archaic; Contact period.
English, the. *See* European explorers; European settlements in the Northeast.
Erosion, 3.
Eskers, 5.
Estuaries,
　as source of food, 29, 32, 51, 82;
　definition of, 29;
　effect of sea level rise on, 29, 32.
European contact. *See* Contact Period.
European description of native farms. *See* Champlain, Samuel de.
European description of native peoples. *See* Wood, William.
European explorers, 85, 87, **90** (map);
　from England, 87;
　from France, 87. *See also* Champlain, Samuel de.
　from Holland (Dutch), 87;
　from Iceland (Norse), 85;
　from Spain, 85, 87. *See also* Columbus, Christopher.
European settlements in the Northeast,
　Dutch, 87, **90** (map);
　English, 87, 90, **90** (map), 102-104;
　failed attempts of, 87;
　French, 87, **90** (map), 103.
European writers about Northeast, 1500s to 1600s, 90, 91, 92. *See also* Bradford, William; Champlain, Samuel de; Wood, William.
Evergreen forests
　at end of Paleo, 19;
　in Early Archaic, 29;
　in Late Archaic, 40;
　in Middle Archaic, **38** (map).
Excavating. *See* Archaeological sites, excavating of.
Explorers. *See* European explorers.

Farming,
　beginning of, in Americas, 60;
　described by Europeans, 91-92;
　in Contact period, 92, **98** (illustr.);
　in eastern North America, 60-62, 72;
　in Northeast, 72;
　in Late Woodland, central New York, 72, 74, **76-77** (illustr.); northern areas, 84; southern areas, 82.
Farming tools, **98** (illustr.).
Finger Lakes, New York, created by glaciers, 5.
Fire making. *See* Strike-a-light; Tools, stone.
Fire pits, 67, 70, 83, 92.
First people in North America, 8-9; theories on arrival of, 9. *See also* Paleo Indians.
Fish, fresh water, 24, 32, 37, 49, 66, 82. *See also* Food; Fishing.
Fish, migratory, 29, 43, 68, 83.
Fish, ocean, and sea mammals. *See also* Fish, migratory.
　in Early Archaic period, 29 (alewives, salmon, shad);
　in Late Archaic Lake Forest, 43 (sea mammals);
　in Late Archaic Maritime, 40, 43 (sea mammals, shellfish, swordfish);
　in Late Archaic southern coasts, 40, 51 (shellfish, clams, crabs, seals);
　in Late Woodland, 83 (shellfish, sturgeon);
　in Middle Archaic, 32, 37 (sea mammals, shellfish);
　in Middle Woodland, 69, 70 (clams, oysters, quahogs, scallops, sea mammals, shellfish).
Fishermen, European, 85. *See also* Contact Period.
Fishing,
　in Contact period, 98;
　in Early Archaic, 29, 31, 32;
　in Early Woodland, 67;
　in Late Archaic, Lake Forest, 48; Maritime, 43; southern coasts, 51, 52, 53, 55; southern forests, 50, 52;
　in Late Woodland, 83, 98;
　in Middle Archaic, 32, **37** (illustr.);
　in Middle Woodland, Maine, 70; Point Peninsula, 67, 68, 69.
Fishing equipment. *See also* Tools, bone or antler; Tools, stone.
　fishing weight, **69** (illustr.);
　harpoons (illustr.), **33, 67, 69, 70, 98;**
　bone hooks, 50, **52** (illustr.); **54** (illustr.), 67;
　nets, 50, 52, 67, 93 (Table);
　netsinker, **52** (illustr.);
　plummets (illustr.), **42, 48, 54, 55;**
　spears, 50, 52, 67;
　weirs, **52-53** (illustr.).
Flax, 98.
Flint corn. *See* Corn.
Flute, 49, 50. *See also* Musical instruments.
Fluted point. *See* Spear points, Paleo.
Food. *See also* listings by specific food; Crops; Farming; Fish; Fruit; Hunting; Nuts.
　in Contact period, 92, 93, in northern areas, 98;
　in Early and Middle Woodland, 65-67, 72;
　in Early Archaic, 29, **31** (map);
　in Late Archaic, Lake Forest, 43; Maritime, 40, 43; southern areas, 49; southern coasts, 51;
　in Late Woodland, 82;
　in Middle Archaic, 32, 37;
　in Middle Woodland, interior forests, 67; Maine, 70; southern coasts, 67-70;
　in Paleo, 9, 19, 24.

Food preparation. *See also* Tools, stone.
  boiling, in pottery, 62, 67, 74, **92** (illustr.), 98; in metal pots, 102;
  grinding, with mortar and pestle (illustr.), **50, 54, 55, 83**;
  pit baking, 83;
  roasting, 49;
  stone boiling, 58.
Food storage, 49; in pits, 65, 66, 67, 70, 72, 83.
Forests. *See also* Birch trees; Evergreen forests; Hemlocks; Oak forests; Pine trees.
  Early Archaic, 29, 31;
  Late Archaic, northern coast, 40;
  Middle Archaic, 32, **38** (map);
  Paleo, 18-19.
Foxes, Late Archaic, northern areas, 40.
French, the. *See* Champlain, Samuel de; European explorers; European settlements in the Northeast.
Frogs, as food, 32. *See also* Food, Middle Archaic.
Frontenac Island, New York (Lake Forest Archaic site), 43-48, 49.
Fruits. *See also* Food.
  in Contact period, 93 (Table);
  in Lake Forest Archaic, 43, 65, 67.
Fur trade. *See* Trade, with Europeans.

Game animals. *See individual animals*; Food; Hunting; Ice Age animals.
Games, 50.
Geese, 43.
Geologists. *See* Scientists, who work with archaeologists.
Georges Bank, 14, **15** (maps).
Glacial drift, 3. *See also* Glaciers.
Glacial environment, 5, **8-9** (illustr.), 13. *See also* Tundra.
Glaciers, 3-13. *See also* Ice Age.
  changes caused by, 3, 5;
  description of, 3;
  effect of, on sea-level, 8;
  effect of, on weather, 5;
  landforms created by, 3-5.
Gorget (illustr.), **66, 69**.
Gouge (illustr.), **33, 42, 48, 54, 82**. *See also* Tools, stone, woodworking.
Gourds, 60, 72, 98.
Grapes, 67, 93 (Table). *See also* Food, Middle Woodland.
Green Mountains, 3.
Grid. *See* Archaeological sites, excavating of.
Groundnuts, 98. *See also* Food.

Hairstyles, 90-91.
Harpoon, toggling. *See* L'Anse Amour (site).
Harpoons. *See* Fishing equipment.
Health, native population's
  before European contact, 90-91;
  after European contact, 102.
Hemlocks, 19, 29. *See also* Forests.
Hickory nuts, 49. *See also* Nuts.
Hideworking. *See* Tools, stone.
Hispaniola, 85.
Hopewell people, 65; influence on Northeastern culture, 66.
  *See also* Trade.

Houses,
  in Contact period, **92** (illustr.);
  in Early Woodland, New York, Scaccia, 66;
  in Late Archaic, Lake Forest, Frontenac Island, 48; Lake Forest, Lamoka Lake, **50** (illustr.); southern coasts, Wapanucket 6, **58** (illustr.);
  in Late Woodland, northern Maine, 84; southern New England (wigwams), **82** (illustr.); upstate New York (longhouses), 74-**75** (illustr.);
  in Middle Woodland, Maine (pit-houses), 70-71; Martha's Vineyard, 70; New York, Point Peninsula, 67;
  in Paleo, **8-9**, **22-23** (illustr.), lack of evidence, 19.
Hudson, Henry, 87.
Hudson River valley,
  created by glaciers, 5;
  in Late Woodland, 76-77;
  trade routes in, **89** (map).
Hunting. *See also* Tools, stone.
  in Contact period, in northern areas, 98;
  in Early Archaic, 32;
  in Late Archaic, 40;
  in Late Woodland, 72, **98** (illustr.);
  in Middle Archaic, 32, 38;
  in Paleo, **12** (illustr.).

Ice Age, **4** (map). *See also* Glaciers.
  changes in plant and animal life in, 18-19, 28;
  definition of, 3;
  end of, in Northeast, 18-19;
  last, 3, 5-8, 13, 14-**15** (maps).
Ice Age animals, **8-9** (illustr.), 19, disappearance of, 28, 29.
Ice-free corridor, **4** (map), 8. *See also* Glaciers.
Iceland, explorers from, 85.
Ice sheets. *See also* Glaciers.
  last, in North America, **4** (map), 5-6;
  last, in Northeast, 14-**15** (maps);
  location in Early Archaic period, 29.
Indian, derivation of word, 85.
Iroquois, 72, 76, 92, 103; annual cycle, **94-95** (illustr.).
Iroquois Confederacy, 76, 92, relationship with the English and French, 103.

Kames, 5. *See also* Glaciers.
Kennebec River, site of rock carving at, 99.
Kettle holes, 5, in Northeast, 18. *See also* Glaciers.
Kettle ponds. *See* Kettle holes.
Kettles, metal (European), 87, 98, 102. *See also* Trade, with Europeans.
Kidnapping of native people, by English, 87; by Portuguese, 85.
King Phillip's War, 103.
Kipp Island, New York (Middle Woodland, Point Peninsula site), 69.

Labrador sites (maps), **30, 41, 61**. *See also* L'Anse Amour.
Lake Albany, 14-**15** (maps). *See also* Glaciers.
Lake Champlain. *See also* Champlain Sea.
  Early Woodland sites on, 66-67, Boucher, Vermont, 68;
  in glacial times, 5, 14-**15** (maps);
  in Late Woodland, 76, 77;
  Late Archaic trade on, 65, 66.

New York, 49-51;
 Late Woodland, 74-76, **78-79** (illustr.), 82;
  palisaded, **93**, **98** (illustr.).
Vinette I. *See* Pottery, earliest.


Walden Pond, 18.
Wampanoag tribe today, 104.
Wampum, 93, 98, **99** (illustr.).
Wapanucket 6, Massachusetts, Late Archaic site, **58** (illustr.).
Warfare, 75, 98.
Wars, with Europeans, 103.
Weapons. *See* Bow and arrow; Spear points.


Weather, during Pleistocene, 5.
Weirs. *See* Boylston Street Fish Weirs, Fishing equipment,
 weirs.
West Athens Hill, New York, Paleo site, **26** (illustr.).
Whale effigy, **43** (illustr.).
Whales, 82. *See also* Food, Early Woodland.
White Mountains, 3.
Whistle, Early Woodland, Meadowood, **66** (illustr.); Middle
 Archaic, from L'Anse Amour, **39** (illustr.).
Wigwam, **82** (illustr.), 83, interior of, **92** (illustr.). *See also*
 Houses, Late Woodland.
Wild plants, uses of, 93 (Table).
Wood, William,
 English writer, 90;
 description of Native people by, 90-91.
Woodland period, 60-84;
 divisions, 60;
 Early, 62-67;
 Middle, 67-71;
 Late, 72-84.
Woodworking. *See* Tools, stone.
Writing, in New World, 2.
Written records. *See* Record of the past, written.

# About the Authors

**Esther K. Braun** did her undergraduate work at Wellesley College before receiving an M.A. in Education from Northeastern University. She is a retired teacher from the Lincoln (Massachusetts) Public Schools who specialized in math, science, and Social Studies. The *First Peoples of the Northeast* was inspired by her experience in the classroom, where she sought appropriate and accurate resource materials on the topic. This is her first collaboration with her son.

**David P. Braun** followed undergraduate studies at Harvard University with M.A. and Ph.D. degrees in Anthropology from the University of Michigan. A specialist in North American archaeology, emphasizing the midwest and northeast, Dr. Braun has published numerous articles in professional journals and contributed to thirteen books. He has served as an Associate Professor of Anthropology at Southern Illinois University, as Director of Publications for the Center for Archaeological Investigations at Southern Illinois University, as a Fellow of the School of American Research in Santa Fe, and as an Adjunct Professor of Anthropology at Northern Arizona University. Following his career in archaeology, Dr. Braun received an M.S. in Water Resources Administration from the University of Arizona and is currently a Hydrologist with The Nature Conservancy.